Leaving Home at 83

SANDRA BUTLER

RATTLING GOOD YARNS
PRESS

Rattling Good Yarns Press
33490 Date Palm Drive 3065
Cathedral City CA 92235
USA
www.rattlinggoodyarns.com

Cover Design: Rattling Good Yarns Press

Library of Congress Control Number: 2024943926
ISBN: 978-1-955826-66-2

First Edition

To my daughters Janaea McAlee and Alison Butler, who kept me afloat during this complicated time with patience and love. I am forever grateful.

Contents

Part One
Leaving Home

One
A Failed Birthday Wish

My eighty-third birthday began with a party, then went steadily downhill at 100 miles an hour. I had flown to Phoenix, where my ex-husband was in an assisted living facility being looked after by our two daughters and my son-in-law. We would all gather to ceremonially usher me into the year ahead, one that quickly went from not bad at all, to all the way terrible.

They had arranged for my birthday lunch in an extravagant restaurant. Big dinners that begin at 7:00 are no longer an option for my aging digestive system. Since their dad's diet consists of Ensure, one martini, vanilla ice cream, and soup, lunch it was. While mascara and cute shoes had not been a part of my lesbian clothing choices for decades, I made "an effort," which included darkening my eyelashes with an ancient wand of mascara, putting on earrings, and what I thought of as my cute shoes which pinched my toes, resulting in my walking with a series of sudden lurches.

We settled at an outdoor table nestled in a grotto of carefully manicured foliage, surrounded by people wearing insistent shades of salmon and periwinkle, emerald, and lemon, thus increasing the price of our lunch a hundred-fold. Wally ordered his daily martini and beamed at us. He could no longer hear what was being said nor would he have remembered it if he had, but he was happy we were all together. Our children integrated the responsibilities of his continuing decline into their busy lives, and seeing how much attention and patience this required of them, my private blowing-out-the-birthday-candles wish was that they wouldn't have to integrate me any time soon.

The year looked full of possibilities since the worst of COVID appeared to be lifting. I had been vaccinated and boosted, and while mask-wearing was still necessary for indoor spaces, I wouldn't be as locked in as I had been for the past year. I was looking forward to a good spring.

It wasn't. And the summer was worse.

My children had noticed my increasing dry cough and shortness of breath in our Zoom conversations over the past few months. I'd been pretending this was no big deal, which was taking an increasing amount of anxiety-fueled energy.

"Just check it out, Mom," they sternly instructed before I left to return to California. Grudgingly yielding to their concerns, I did.

After a thorough exam, my doctor ordered a CT scan, which led to a quickly scheduled PET scan, followed by a biopsy a few days later. My eighty-third year began with days of lying still on a series of cold pallets while machines buzzed and whirred over my body and technicians moved around briskly, flashing professional smiles as I tried to read the expression on their unchanging neutral faces.

In an unsettling coincidence, my primary care physician had also identified a large squamous cell carcinoma that had taken up residence alongside my nose. It was big and deep enough that a surgeon would have to dig down into my face to get it out. A MOHRS surgery was scheduled.

Three days later, my cheek had been excavated and sutured with ten stitches, leaving me looking like a poorly made-up Phantom of the Opera. As I was returning to the parking lot, my cell phone rang.

"Your cancer isn't a big one. We caught it early. We'll take it out, put it in a bucket, and throw it away," the surgeon said warmly, in an image presumably designed to be reassuring. Visualizing a metal pail with pieces of me sloshing around didn't get me anywhere near the degree of reassurance she intended, although I appreciated her trying.

Her words sounded tinny as I held the phone to the good side of my face. Two cancers in one day! What are the odds of that? I had lung cancer. Needing surgery. At once. It was staged as a 1A3, a small tumor, that hadn't spread to any nearby lymph nodes. While it certainly wasn't the worst diagnosis I might have received, it was most decidedly—something.

All my friends already had had something. Several of them had had several somethings: breast cancer, strokes, MS, COPD, epilepsy, falls accompanied by a slow recovery, as well as all the inevitable knee and hip replacements. Decades before, I had been diagnosed with thyroid cancer which had been resolved by removing the offending organ and replacing it with medication that tricked my body into thinking it was still there. It wasn't a big deal—as big deals go. But until now, it had been my biggest deal. Not counting my knee replacements which were straightforward surgeries. They were just parts of my body that had dried up. Now, I would join the legions of women with something.

The first order of business was telling my family and friends. I rehearsed my words, wanting to acknowledge the reality of my cancer without making it too big a deal, especially with friends who had or were still navigating even bigger deals than mine.

I broke the news to my daughters like Joe Friday in *Dragnet*: Just the facts, ma'am. Not that I thought I was fooling them. They had their lives. They had their dad. And, against all my best intentions, they now had me. This would just be temporary. Surgery. Recovery and back to my life. I didn't want them to have to incorporate me. Not yet.

Janaea, my eldest, reacted with concern about how I felt. She sent flowers and cards and love. Alison researched lung cancer, staging, video-assisted lobectomy, recovery, life span statistics, and everything she would need to take care of me. After years of managing the medical and emotional realities of their dad's life, they had developed a way of dividing and sharing the responsibilities. Alternating visits. Taking him for drives when he was up to it. Consulting with medical staff. Supplying Depends and Ensure, creating drawings to explain how the TV remote worked, being sure there was ice cream, and litter for the kitty that kept him company. They each took on different parts of what was required to support the diminishing life of an old man. Now Alison would handle my post-surgical care, and Janaea would take full responsibility for their dad and shower me with long-distance devotion. My birthday wish was a bust.

Telling my friends was easier because we had already managed many more serious illnesses. We knew how this went. The 1A3 would require rides to the doctor, casseroles, visits, and love. They would provide that. Alison would be there to hold everything together.

Swimming just under the surface, of course, were my feelings, which were escaping their carefully imposed bondage, becoming more insistent, erupting in terrifying dreams of home invasion and assault. It didn't take much to interpret myself. Someone was going to enter my body and take one of the five lobes of my lungs. But I was an adult, and an eighty-three-year-old adult at that, who needed to handle this. I took charge of my anxiety with a yellow pad writing SURGERY at the top and underlining it firmly. On the first line, I wrote WHEELCHAIR.

Years before, upon my return from my second knee replacement, confident I could navigate the long corridor to my apartment using my newly issued crutches, my certainty turned out to be misguided, and less than halfway down the hall, I slid to the floor, my determination sturdier than my strength. I only managed to get into my bed after the friend who was accompanying me left me splayed in the hall, went to my apartment, retrieved my desk chair, wrestled me into it, and rolled me the rest of the way. Now my first attempt to exert control over this new diagnosis and my fear was to rent a wheelchair to navigate my return from a surgery that had not yet even been scheduled.

My list expanded, each item augmenting my precarious sense of stability. Fill freezer. Restock the medicine cabinet. Create a schedule of friends for visits, casseroles, and love. Buy a pretty new bathrobe. And of course, have a pedicure.

My television viewing, which usually functioned as a source of relaxation at the end of the day, changed. Police procedurals with people running from danger, and medical ones with people dying from both rare and ordinary diseases were all now off the table. I needed undemanding, soothing distractions, shows that would allow the minutes to pass while I held myself steady. I returned to my early years, a complicated time to be sure, but not one where I had lung cancer. I watched Judy Garland grow up, William Powell and Myrna Loy banter, knock back martinis and solve crimes, Fred and Ginger dance, and Rita Hayworth be sultry. My reading was an immersion into Louise Penny's series about Three Pines. There were murders, an extraordinary number of murders for such a small town, but both the environment and the locals were loving and benign, so I knew all would eventually be well. I very much needed everything to eventually be well.

The doctors had instructed me to walk as far and as vigorously as my lungs would permit to get them in the best possible shape for the lobectomy. Since one lobe would be removed, the other four would have to work overtime to compensate. It was a goal and a focus that motivated me to be an active participant in this process. Not a patient. A participant. I got myself up to eleven thousand steps a day, marching around the marina near my apartment, chin thrust out like the prow of a ship as I walked myself into exhaustion.

The night before the operation I took a final stroll by the water to say farewell to my once sturdy old vessel and appreciate all it had provided me for the past eighty-three years. Returning to my apartment, I had little left to do except walk around, pick things up, then put them down. Move a plant from one table to the next, then return it to where it had looked better. Alison watched my aimless, restless wandering with a quiet kindness. Now I'd have to make friends with a different body, creakier perhaps, slower probably, but still mine. And still deserving my full friendship. That was the plan anyhow.

Two
My Practically Nothing

The surgery proceeded uneventfully, but after the anesthesia began to wear off, my four remaining lobes had to work their behinds off (do lobes have behinds?) to compensate for their missing sister, who had been cut out and thrown unceremoniously to slosh around in a pail.

The number of pills I had to take was a visible reminder of how much attention and help my body needed to recover. I had black and blue blotches left to mark the spots where the three IVs had been stuck in my arms, and angry scars on my side where the incisions had been made. Only the splendid pedicure I got added a touch of insouciance to the otherwise crummy terrain.

I was weak, breathless, sore, in urgent need of a shampoo, and needed three different inhalers to keep my breathing and heart functioning at the right tempo. But I was cared for, and on the road to either recovery or Bali, depending on which Bob Hope movie surfaced in my oxycontin-fueled associations.

Improvement became measured by my ability to enjoy an everything bagel, walk eight hundred and seventeen steps, and ingest massive amounts of turmeric and ginger, although I no longer remember what function it was supposed to serve. Something, I suspect, about general good-for-you-ness.

Then, because the chance of atrial fibrillation is increased when old people have anesthesia, I accommodated the statistics by having such an increase. In the middle of the night, of course, when all emergencies happen. Four very young, very muscular people in uniforms seemed to appear at my bedside (Alison called them), and after asking me some questions and measuring what they described as my "numbers," bundled me off to the emergency room.

After a night spent hallucinating from the dose of fentanyl they gave me, my numbers eventually dropped back into the right neighborhood. I was given a referral for little pads that would be stuck all over my chest and worn for thirty days to determine if I had Afib, or if the combination of the surgery and my oldness had been the culprit. Now, I would have to relearn to breathe, walk, and even talk—all at once. I bought an Apple watch, which my daughters convinced me to get as an alternative to a necklace that broadcasts, "I fell, and I can't get up." A watch, I decided, was infinitely more stylish. And private. I programmed it with all the emergency bells and whistles to relieve their concerns.

The doctor had taken an entire lobe out of my lung and what was left was learning to function without its lobe mate. But how breathless was I? Was it a good day or an ominous one? Should I lie down and just wait it out? Could I be having another episode? What did OK breathlessness feel like? I repeatedly pressed the watch's heart icon to keep track of my fluctuations, attributing fearful meanings to how my lungs were learning to function in this new configuration.

All this insistent pressing and counting, gauging, and assessing happened in a world where the tail end of the COVID quarantine kept me inside. Massive wildfires all over California were making the air unbreathable and entire towns were going up in flames. My windows were tightly closed, and a machine filtered and purified the air as the sky outside turned orange with pollution. People were losing their homes as I huddled inside worriedly and repeatedly pressing my Apple watch heart icon. My sense of vulnerability was coming from every direction. But I was only a 1A3. My cancer was practically nothing. But it was my practically nothing.

Eventually the morning Alison was to return to Phoenix arrived. She stood in the doorway and began the "review," something we do in our family when whoever provided caregiving after an illness is leaving. It begins with, "Remember to..." and then cascades down the list of medications, exercises, mental health advice, resources, and what's in the freezer. It's our way of saying goodbye.

"I will love. I'll do everything. I promise. Don't worry. I'll be fine. You'll see."

After our third teary embrace, I watched her wheel her suitcase down the hallway toward the elevator. She turned back, waved, and called one more "I love you" in my direction as I produced a cheerful smile before she turned the corner and was out of sight. I turned to enter the newly empty apartment and gathered up the remnants of her presence, the scattering of toothpicks, empty stevia packets, pillows, a forgotten sock, her toothbrush on the edge of the sink. I was alone now with whatever came next.

Three
Privately Cranky, Publicly Plucky

Three days later, my knee exploded, ballooning to three times the size of a standard knee. Now, I was both breathless and needed crutches. Transporting my morning cup of coffee from the counter to the chair, where I exhaustedly collapsed after accomplishing such a herculean feat, took all the energy I had. My knee wasn't painful unless I tried to stand, so I decided to remain seated and wait for it to resolve on its own. As a result, the necessary steps to get my phone charger, rescue inhaler, thermos of water, iPad, and Tylenol were kept to a bare minimum. This was a big no-no. I was supposed to move as much as I could. My lungs needed me to move. But my knee and I were sitting. Waiting to resolve.

After two days of patting my knee encouragingly, hoping it would return to itself, I gave in and called the hospital's Orthopedic Department. I wanted an answer, and to get one in Kaiser's massive system—I decided to be super dramatic. I LIVE ALONE. I COULD FALL. I JUST HAD SURGERY. I HAD A BIG AFIB EPISODE.

It worked. Someone would be able to see me later that day. After a brief exam, they explained that my swelling was caused by the medication I took to manage the side effects of Afib. There was one pill to treat the symptoms of Afib and a second to treat the side effects of the first. It was the latter that caused my knee explosion.

They altered my cocktail of pills, reducing the danger of my knee swelling again, but raising the concern of another Afib episode. In my mind, I had had an exploded knee and an attack of arrhythmia. Exploding and attacking, the language of war, best described what was happening in my body now.

The following weekend, the fire alarm went off. A recorded voice, male, of course, boomed into every apartment at one-minute intervals. Attention. Attention. There is an emergency in the building. Please leave the building. Do not use the elevators. Then repeat. And repeat. But without the elevators, there was no way I could get down four flights of stairs. I sat in my chair hoping it wasn't a real fire because if it was, I was a goner. The recording continued for nearly twenty minutes as I visualized fingers of flames beginning to creep under my door, my heart rate ballooning like my knee.

Eventually, the fire department arrived and determined someone had burned their dinner. The loudspeaker announcement switched to the reassuring "return to your homes." I pushed myself out of my chair, tucked my crutches under my arms, and made my eager way to the freezer, where Alison had thoughtfully left me several pints of rum raisin for emergencies. This had been an emergency. I ate the entire pint.

At the end of the month, the numbers that emerged from the pads covering my chest confirmed that my body had reacted to anesthesia as senior bodies often do. I didn't have Afib. I was just old. The medication was stopped, and my knee eventually returned to the size that matched up with its partner.

Every morning, my downstairs neighbor came upstairs to sit just outside the bathroom door while I showered. Not that it was a real shower. It was me sitting on a chair using a handheld faucet. But I was naked and weak and exposed and wet, and knowing she was nearby provided a welcome sense of comfort.

I still couldn't go outside under my own steam but made "squares" around my apartment hallway corridors with my Lamborghini, which was an appreciatively pretentious name for my new red rollator. It was cuter than a walker because it had a padded seat so I could stop and rest as much as I needed to, which was a lot.

After one, then two weeks of lumbering around the apartment and the hallways, I began to wonder if my days of living independently might be coming to an end. I knew I could count on friends for medical appointments, meals, and visits. But laundry? Emergencies in the middle of the night? Shopping? Not a big shopping, just an out-of-milk shopping. While they were all quick to offer help and support, most were tucked into partnered lives, and our now middle-aged children had moved back into the mix. They were newly worried about how we were living our oldness, which was alternately annoying and welcome. Their advice was freely offered often long before it was requested. Nothing was the way it used to be. Not only were children insisting on a voice in our lives, but partners were becoming dilapidated and needing more attention. The foundation hadn't just shifted—it had crumbled. We were all a big loving mess.

Years before, we had promised one another to be "there" as we aged, but the precise location of "there" kept moving out of reach. These women who had become my chosen family were not going to be able to "take me through," nor was I going to be able to take them anywhere at all. For the first time since I was eight years old, I was unable to cross the street on my own. I wanted to return to the time before my body insisted I pay attention to it. Before the pandemic, before the wildfires, before Trump, and especially before cancer.

The doctors were right. Eventually, I did get stronger, my breathing steadied, and I could walk further, although still accompanied by the reassurance of my rollator. I even began to drive again. I remained privately cranky but publicly plucky. I made the bed and rested. I brushed my teeth and rested. I changed the sheets and rested. While it was reassuring to have my friends exclaiming about how well I was doing, as I bobbed my head modestly, I didn't tell them that I was lonely. I wanted them to see me as resolute. I didn't want a pep talk, suggestions, or to cause them concern, because there was nothing they could do except love me, which they were already doing. I worried that I was postponing the inevitable, adapting to what was possible going forward, rather than being proactive and creating a life that would be a better fit for my tired body and weary heart. My surgery was in the rearview mirror physically, but emotionally things were going from hard to grim.

Four
Hoping to Be A Welcome Burden

My oldest friend was in the hospital for the third time in less than a month. Everything was wrong. Her lungs. Her heart. Her kidneys. All her systems were shutting down.

Marcia and I met forty years ago and became friends at once. She loved to tell people we were in a Boston marriage, a centuries-old description of a long-term primary, yet platonic relationship between two unmarried women. We were indeed in a marriage of sorts, even as we had our own lovers, adventures, travels, family life, and political priorities. We had accompanied one another through four decades, and now she was dying.

I had read about anticipatory grief. I had lost beloveds before. But in this depleted moment, I was unprepared to live with the crushing reality of her absence. I was in mourning for her impending death, for my once undemanding body, and for a political world that seemed to be careening out of control. While I could still drive at night, avoid leaving the stove on and the computer off, and remember most things with the growing exception of intermittent nouns, I knew there would come a time when each of those capacities would fall away. Then, eventually, so would I. Where did I want to be during that inevitable slow dissolve?

I know, I thought. *I'll move.* The old geographic solution. I'll live in a senior residence where I'll be cared for and feel more secure. Yet every self-help book that has ever been written tells the reader in the firmest of tones NEVER to make a major life decision after a death or a significant life change. I had even read some of those books.

Wait, they caution. Let the disruption of those life events settle a bit, before considering what's next. But after spending more than a year alone during COVID, punctuated only by failed efforts at yelling across a six-foot space trying to have a conversation with a masked person and unable to hear their reply, when I couldn't put my arms around my friends for an embrace because I'd risk contacting germs, when one beloved was moving towards the end of her life, and another had just received a terminal diagnosis, and when my body seemed to be giving up whatever ghost it had managed to keep intact for eighty-three years, I needed to make a major life decision. It was the only autonomy I had left.

The webbing that had held my life together was evaporating. My apartment urgently needed to be repainted after years of living with faded and stained apartment house standard-issue beige walls. I wanted to be repainted too. Refreshed. I wanted to recreate the self that eagerly carried my brand-new number two pencil box to the Edith C. Baker school every September. I wanted newness. Beginnings. These endings were too painful. The death of friends. The disruption of my body. The year of isolation. The exhaustion of being a good sport through all of it. Finding if not a silver lining, then at least a newly painted beige one.

Of course, wherever I went, if I remained in the country, there would be chaos. My friends would still sicken and die. And my body would continue its decline. Moving from one state to another wouldn't derail that speeding train. That's why the books tell you not to make decisions.

As a woman who has been devoted to books all her life, a woman who has written them and learned from them, I disregarded their warnings. I contacted The Redwoods, a nearby retirement community with glorious views and lots of old lefties. Meals. Cleaning. 24/7 on-call nurse. Near my friends. It would have been perfect. Except it wasn't. There were no openings, which meant no one was dying. I could pay to get on a waiting list which meant being fourth in line for a one-bedroom, otherwise known as four deaths. Deaths with studios wouldn't move me up on the list. The Redwoods weren't going to work.

But I was on a roll. I was being proactive. Shaping my own future. Not being a passive bystander to the vagaries of my body. This next step, cautioned against by the books, was an even bolder decision than moving from one side of the Bay Area to the other. I'd go all the way to Phoenix!

I had known too many mothers who had put their wobbly foot down, and told their middle-aged children in no uncertain terms that they had no intention of becoming a burden to them. They concluded their declaration by promising not to slip, fall, drive at night and whatever other minor acquiescence the frustrated child could wrest from their insistent parent. They would remain in their own homes, often several states or a continent away. This outcome meant that the children, or at least the children who were able, had to drive or fly for dozens of hours to get to the aging parent who had fallen, forgotten, been diagnosed with something, or had simply sprained their ankle and couldn't get up the stairs. This was, for my money, becoming a distinct burden.

I wasn't going to be one of those old women who didn't know when to quit, who fought to hold onto her independence, downplayed her growing limitations, and was too fearful to leave a life that was familiar and comfortable. Who suffered her child's irritated scolding because she lost something or forgot something or repeated herself. All of which I already did. Especially the repeating.

I'd sacrifice my autonomy, acknowledge my body was going to continue to demand increasing time, medications, doctors, vitamins, rest and kindness. I assuaged my fears by convincing myself that I was moving to Phoenix to protect my daughters from having to disrupt their lives as my body continued to age and need attention. Not that I was apprehensive about what might be my future, and wanted the reassurance of being near them.

The time had come for me to take the next step before I no longer had a choice. The timing, I assured myself, was auspicious. My daughters wouldn't have to integrate me into their daily lives as they had their dad. They'd brought him from his life in New York after he was no longer able to live on his own. I'd witnessed how stressful and demanding the physical and emotional process had been, both for him and our daughters. I wouldn't put them through that again, so if, or more likely when, another "something" happened, they'd be nearby, and I wouldn't disrupt their lives. Or, at least, I hoped, not too much. Nothing that would qualify as my becoming a burden.

But in creating the narrative that cast me as a generous, loving mother who was making difficult decisions for the future well-being of her children, I was actually protecting myself. I didn't tell my daughters that I was scared and wanted to live near them. I felt too ashamed of my vulnerability. After all, my lung cancer was only a 1A3. I was being foolish and would probably be fine. But after COVID, after my surgery, after the wildfires, after my inability to function under my own steam, and after the comfort of having Alison in the next room, I wanted to be with her. With Janaea. With mine. My chosen family had held my life for more than forty-five years. Now, I wanted my children.

They had thoroughly researched all the residential senior living complexes years before when they moved their dad. I asked if they thought any of them might be a good fit for me, and there appeared to be two options. The Wildwoods was too expensive, so Desert Manor it was. It was affordable compared to some of the more elaborately landscaped amenity-rich, serene, out-of-the-center-of-town communities.

There was a two-bedroom apartment with a large balcony on the top floor that was available, and after living in a one-bedroom for decades, having extra space for a proper office—although I didn't yet know exactly what I'd be doing in said office—seemed persuasive. I watched the promotional video and it ticked off all my boxes. It was near the girls, and while it was on a busy thoroughfare, it was set back far enough, it seemed, so that traffic noises wouldn't be an issue. I can't hear when I take out my hearing aids anyway. There was a daily schedule of activities, although I didn't examine that category nearly as closely as I should have.

And there were meals. I would never again have to shop, cook, clean up, and do it all again just a few hours later. That was the part of being an adult I enjoyed the least. I would be fed. I wanted to be fed. Of course, I didn't know that then. But a spacious dining room overlooking a rolling lawn with waitstaff to bring my meals seemed both luxurious and comforting. I was, however, allowed only two meals, required to choose between lunch or dinner. Breakfast was served in the café, and lunch and/or dinner were served either in the café from warming trays or, more formally, in the dining room.

"I'll take it," I told them.

"But don't you want to come and look at it?" Janaea asked.

"We'll see," the answer I always gave when I didn't know how to decide.

But we didn't see. I was caught between not wanting to be a burden and wanting to be taken care of, which left my daughters scrambling to navigate the only choice I had given them. We never talked about my getting an apartment of my own, or moving a little further away from the middle of the city. We never talked about anything.

Five
Leaving My Life Behind

I turned to my tried-and-true way forward with a yellow pad and Sharpies to begin the process of dismantling my home. I started with the ugly presents that had accumulated in the back of the linen closet. While I was careful to put them out on the coffee table when the giver of said gift was visiting, I returned them to the shadowy recesses of the closet as soon as they left. They were all donated.

I would be moving to the desert, so winter coats and heavy sweaters would be superfluous. Hiking boots, too, since I no longer did anything approximating hiking. Walking was my speed now. Everything that no longer fit my changing body was taken to Community Thrift. That included anything with waists or without sleeves. And how many candlesticks did anyone need to have? The mid-century dining table, originally my mother's, then mine for the past twenty-five years, was too big and no longer necessary. I wasn't going to entertain. I wasn't even going to cook. Once the center of a room filled with dinner parties, rich conversations, quiet coffee dates, a desk for my overflow papers, and a spot where I could just sit and look out at the water moving past my window, the table would now become a part of another family's future.

Then there were my books. Those decisions were more complicated. My falling-apart Baldwin paperback essays and novels filled with my youthful exclamation marks. The collection of first novels by women who went on to successful writing lives. Memoirs and a wide range of political analyses that had deepened my thinking and understanding of the world. Current novels, books written by friends, and those that represented an interest that had come and gone. But right now, which parts of my history do I want to take forward? What should I do with the texts I used during my decade-long immersion in Jewish study? There were translations of the Tanach, books of interpretation, scriptural analyses, and personal histories as women moved more deeply into leadership, creating feminist liturgy and alternative forms of practice. Many of those books were dusty now. They had served their purpose. Their words had entered me, nourished and guided me. It was time for another seeker to have them. I donated most of my novels, political essays, and analyses to an under-resourced high school library, the religious texts found their new life in a synagogue library, and the rest came with me.

Within weeks, my home was no longer recognizable as I moved through the growing stacks of boxes, rolled-up rugs, plastic cartons and wilted plants. I didn't bother to dust anymore. Or straighten up. Everything was in disarray. Including me. Vases, skillets, and down vests filled the back seat of my car each morning. These were artifacts of a life that was ending. The staff at Community Thrift began to recognize me as I pulled up each morning, laden with the day's donation. Remnants of my life scattered like dandelions carrying my wishes as I blew their petals into the air. Now, my wish was that what I had felt was either indispensable or beautiful would be similarly valued by its next owner.

The decorative objects that were to accompany me were gifts of a pottery Havdalah set and a brass menorah a friend had purchased decades before in Jaffa. The moss green bowl I gave my mother after she had fallen in love with it in a museum art store. The bronze statue of my daughter as a young dancer, the copper jug I bought from a survivor in Yugoslavia during the war. A carefully folded silk handkerchief in an envelope labeled with my mother's handwriting, "This was my mother's." I packed my grandmother's bamboo cane, my mother's cloisonne pill box, and a silver bell she kept by her bed. They represented my memories. I was careful to be sure my daughters knew each item's history because they would be sorting through my things after I died, determining what to keep and what to pass forward, as I did my mother's belongings, and she did hers.

In addition to the emotional labor of sorting through my belongings, I was leaving my women's group that had begun thirty-four years before, when we first gathered to talk about our experiences of menopause and life in our fifties. But within a few months, our conversations expanded to include the politics of health care, the diminishments that accompany aging, adjustments to this new stage of our lives, and, within a few years, everything else. We have been talking about everything else since then. They have become my chosen family. We call ourselves the "mennies" now, all of us decades past menopause. Our meetings still focus on aging, health care, adjustments to this new stage of our lives—and everything else.

I was leaving my godson Evan, with whom I had shared every Thursday night for twelve years. I celebrated my 70th birthday as he was approaching his first, and was given a fairy wand by his mothers, an acknowledgment of the role and the magic they invited me to bring into his life. I was to be his Fairy Sandy.

We had spent dozens of Thursdays entertaining audiences of stuffed animals with Evan as the star, standing on top of the dining room table singing show tunes. I was the master of ceremonies and responsible for telling the animals to turn off their cell phones. I always had a story or adventure prepared for our visit together. When he was old enough to sit in the front seat alongside me, we ventured further afield. Drives where he was in charge of whether we turned left or right, leading us to unfamiliar parts of the city as we drove up and down winding streets, imagining the people in the houses and whether we liked the architecture and colors, and what we thought their lives were like. Now, there is a box labeled "Evan" filled with the drawings and snapshots, the stories we wrote, and the CDs we made. They rest beside all the other boxes filled with my history.

And Marcia was leaving me. She held on until her daughter and granddaughter arrived from Israel, and then after two joyful days with them, she died. One week later, a dozen of her closest friends gathered by the water, scattered her ashes, reminisced, and wept, before turning away to return to our own lives in a world empty of her presence.

Six
Parting the Waters

The movers wheeled the final stack of boxes through my front door and out into the hallway. The contents of my life were now on a truck going to Phoenix. Everything in the empty space looked shabby; there were faded squares on the wall where pictures once hung, and the rooms looked smaller and darker, all the chips and cracks visible. I closed the door for the last time, my house keys inside on the empty countertop. I entered the elevator, exited at the ground floor, and moved through the mail room and out into the parking lot where my Lyft waited. I watched the waters of the Bay and the expansive view of the San Francisco skyline recede, the highway signs pointing us towards the airport, my life in the rearview mirror.

Arriving at the Airport Hilton, I wheeled my overnight bag into the lobby. Everything was on a truck somewhere, on a freeway somewhere, going to a somewhere I'd never seen. What was in my suitcase was as much of me as I would have until the pieces of my life arrived.

The Hilton was a familiar landmark. I had driven past it hundreds of times on my way to pick up a friend on a returning flight. We did that for one another. Picked each other up. When we flew. When we stumbled. When we mourned and when we struggled to find words and needed to be heard. But I was to be picked up in another city, where, at 83, I was to begin again.

Airport hotels are designed to be neutral, a space for transient occupancy. Passengers brought their lives and concerns through these corridors, only to be replaced the next day by others. My room was a space to sleep and then to move on, not a place that carried memory or history. I climbed into the overly large, excessively pillowed bed. It wasn't dark yet, but my day had ended. There was nothing left for me to do. No lists to complete, no calls to make. My Bay Area life was over. Tomorrow would take me forward. I lay in the bed, replaying the moment I had delightedly bought the apartment, had my first dinner party, and met my downstairs neighbor, releasing one chapter and preparing to begin another.

The next morning, I sat at the hotel café table eating the dry scrambled eggs, opened the packets of frozen butter and room temperature preserves, spread them over toast, and sipped mediocre coffee, remembering decades of breakfasts at Betty's, lunches at Saul's, dinners at Renee's. Being an uninterested and inadequate cook, much of my social life was spent visiting with friends in restaurants and eating gourmet meals. Now, my last breakfast was powdered eggs and dry toast. It felt like a punishment for something I didn't know I had done.

I pulled my suitcase to the shuttle stop that would take me to the airport, alone in this liminal space. It was too late to go back, too late to change the outcome of what I had put in motion. The goodbyes had been said. My friends had tried to understand what must have seemed like an unexpected and precipitous choice, but they loved me and supported my decision, even if it undoubtedly bewildered and disappointed them. As the shuttle bus made its way to the Southwest terminal, I held myself still, all the movement outside of me, the wheels turning, the last of the city sliding past the windows.

Two hours later, the plane skidded to a stop on the runway, slowly losing speed as it approached the airport. For the length of the flight, I had been neither here nor there, but moving through space, hovering over my life.

It would soon be Rosh Hashanah, the Jewish New Year, and I hoped this was a good omen for completing one chapter of my life and beginning a new one. I needed some *mazel,* a Hebrew word with a double meaning. It is usually translated to "luck." But it has a second meaning: a favorable constellation of stars. Perhaps the stars were aligning—at least the Jewish stars.

I moved down the narrow aisle to exit the plane, then through the crowded corridors to the street. I stood under the Arrivals sign until Alison's red car pulled up, and as I sank into the seat, she said,

"Welcome to Phoenix, Mom."

It was three months and two weeks after surgery for a 1A3 cancer, after more than a year of COVID quarantine, fires, dangerous air, and isolation, after one friend moved away to New York, and another was diagnosed with advanced esophageal cancer that would soon take her life. After M.'s ashes had entered the sea, after I ignored the advice of all the books that cautioned me against taking this step, I had closed the door of what had been my home for twenty-two years, no longer there and not yet where I was going. Like the Israelites poised at the edge of the Red Sea, trusting it would part and allow them to cross, I was ready to take this step. To trust that the waters would open, and I'd reemerge on dry land. In Phoenix. To pitch my tent in the desert.

The waters did indeed part. And I emerged in the desert. But nothing else was what I had imagined. Not a single thing.

Part Two
Into the Desert

Seven
Into the Desert

I wished my new residence had a better name. I'd left the Watergate, an unprepossessing block of four low-slung apartment buildings that might have been forgettable, except for the fact that they were at the edge of one of the most beautiful waterfronts in the Bay Area. Filled with light and views of San Francisco rising in the background, the Watergate was appropriately named for what and where it was. Now, I was moving to a residential facility called Desert Manor, which evoked either a Las Vegas strip hotel or a gated townhouse complex.

As I waited at Alison's apartment for my furniture to arrive, I rewatched the videos that advertised the multiple benefits of aging at what was to be my new home. Of course, I was aware of marketing strategies about camera angles making small things look bigger (like, as it turned out, the swimming pool). I expected that the grounds would be on prominent display. They were. There were slow scans of the outdoor seating areas, with chairs and tables scattered to represent potential conversational groupings. It was left to the viewer to imagine herself sitting in one of those chairs, surrounded by other residents enjoying the vistas and one another. I did.

The dining room tables were set, and the chandeliers sparkled, allowing me to anticipate the pleasures of having dinner served every night. The food didn't even have to be good. I could be flexible about the quality, as long as the meal was brought to my table and then removed when I was done. That was one of the major selling points of my decision.

Two weeks before my arrival, I chose a paint color that was a rich shade of cream, not the standard pallid beige that covered the walls of every apartment I'd ever had. Janaea bought it, delivered it to the painters, and when they were done, sent me a video of my newly creamy rooms. The walls were terrific, but the rest of the apartment seemed worryingly dark, with small windows providing only a glimpse of the building that housed the assisted living residents. But she was pleased, looking forward to my coming—at least it seemed that way—and I assured her that both the color and she were perfect. I was to live in the independent building since assisted living and memory care, euphemisms for people whose bodies and memory need extra supervision, were on the other side of the campus. Yes, they called it a campus.

My heart sank as soon I entered the building, flanked by my daughters carefully watching my every reaction. This wasn't the upscale hotel lobby that I imagined the video had intended to convey. It was more like an insurance office in a strip mall. We moved into the conventional space, a large desk behind a plastic shield facing us, a scattering of neutral sofas with enthusiastic pillows, and an enormous TV screen mounted on the wall displaying a log burning in a fireplace intended, I assumed, to represent home and hearth.

Approaching the desk, I introduced myself to a woman who was both masked and seated behind the shield. Even with my hearing aids turned up to their highest frequency, there was no way I was going to be able to hear anything she said. My inability to communicate with masked people had been repeatedly confirmed by the pandemic. I turned to Alison who immediately understood my silent communication and stepped forward to talk to her. They murmured together for a while, and then I was given a few papers to sign, pledging my fealty to their rules. I wrote the check that bound me to them for the next year unless, of course, I died. Janaea was given a packet of information, which were, in reality, the rules I would be required to adhere to, enthusiastically titled *Welcome to Desert Manor*.

We passed through the reception area into a cavernous room with a square bar at its center, which could if needed, seat forty people. Shelves displayed generic objects bought in bulk lots, vases, triptychs, and random massive bowls. Televisions were mounted on two sides of the bar, and the stools were filled with a dozen people who were having wine or beer, watching a game, or chatting. Nobody looked like a lesbian, but I wasn't entirely sure what I was expecting old lesbians in Phoenix to look like.

Alongside the bar was a small cafe with a few scattered tables and chairs where people who neither drank nor approved of people who did gathered, marking their displeasure by those few purposeful yards of distance. Behind the cafe was the entrance to the dining room framed by an open shelf upon which were displayed plastic replicas of the day's three dinner choices.

Just beyond the bar and the cafe was a large open area with a piano and pool table at its center before narrowing into a hallway leading to the apartments. Outside the door behind the cafe was the swimming pool, big enough for one baby elephant or three old people to stand in, but not big enough for real swimming. I don't play pool, and my piano playing, while once mediocre, had deteriorated from that low bar. I was moving from nervous to dispirited.

Taking the elevator to the third floor, we walked down the brown linoleum hallway designed to look like wood. It didn't. My apartment was in the Jewish Quarter, so named, I later learned, because of Shana, a resident whose Jewish-themed paintings covered both sides of the mushroom-colored walls. Beside each front door was a shelf designed to provide the residents with an opportunity to express their individuality, make a statement about who they were, or a changing announcement of the holidays they celebrated. We passed artwork that signaled here lives lovers of Brooklyn, Christ, Israel, and grandchildren.

Arriving at my apartment, I found it was, as the videos had indicated, spacious, the living room opening onto a large balcony I was to share with an extended family of pigeons. What the videos had carefully left out was the fact that the pigeons used it as an outhouse. There was pigeon shit everywhere, and undoubtedly, lots more to come. All the shit and the dominant view of the rooftops of neighboring houses put an end to my fantasies of watching the sun rise and set, having morning coffee, and reading in the late afternoon. The pigeons had already claimed the territory.

There were two bathrooms, which were superfluous since I only used one toilet at a time, and the kitchen was the size of a postage stamp. While part of my reason for moving was so that I no longer had to shop, prepare meals, or clean ever again, it was very small and very dark. The countertops were covered in a brown spatter design, but at least the walls were wonderfully creamy. That was something.

Janaea's phone dinged. She looked down at her screen and said,

"They're here, Mom. The movers are downstairs. Alison and I will go down and direct them. OK?"

"Sounds perfect, love." I smiled and continued smiling until they left. Looking around, I told myself that I had made my bed and would sleep in it. Uncomplainingly. I had already disrupted my daughter's life enough. And *that* would be *that* I concluded sternly.

Eventually, the bed I had vowed to uncomplainingly sleep in was delivered, along with all the boxes, sofas, bookcases, pictures, and everything else that constituted my belongings.

"Here." "Over there." "In the other room" was the extent of my depleted vocabulary for the next several hours.

The mover's final task was to set up my bed, but as they began, I noticed hurried whispering among the exhausted men. It appeared a necessary screw had been lost, one of the six that was to hold the mattress frame together. Echoing my surgeon, who tossed a lobe of my lung into a bucket, they assured me that the other five screws were sufficient, that this one didn't matter, that the bed would hold, and not to worry.

"OK," I said wearily, too tired to worry and eager for them to leave.

"Thank you, guys."

My daughters followed me around the apartment for a bit longer after they left, as I opened and closed cabinets and closet doors, reassuring them about how comfortably I would settle in. They made sure I had unpacked soap and toothpaste, made my bed, shook my morning vitamins into a small container, and kissed me goodbye. I didn't act upon my overwhelming impulse to leave with them. I showered, pulled on my sleep tee shirt, and gingerly lowered myself into the bed. It didn't fall apart. I did.

Eight
Inauspicious Beginnings

Further confirmation that my precipitously optimistic choice to move to Desert Manor was not going to work out as I had hoped became apparent the following evening.

Having eaten an egg salad sandwich and several apples throughout the day, at 6:00, a reasonable hour, I thought, for a meal, I took off my unpacking shirt, which was not to be worn anywhere in the vicinity of public space, substituted a more attractive one and went downstairs for my first opportunity to be served dinner. As I approached the entry to the large, crowded dining room, the woman who was there, I assumed to seat residents, looked startled, excused herself, and walked hastily towards the swinging doors to the kitchen. *How lovely*, I thought. They probably have something special for the inaugural meal of new residents. Maybe there will be a cupcake or something festive. She returned, possibly crestfallen, although I couldn't be sure because her mask precluded interpretation, to tell me that the kitchen was closing. I could no longer be served, but she'd be happy to prepare a plate for me to take back to my apartment. The guide to everything you want to know that had been warmly pressed into my hand at the front desk stated clearly that dinner was served from 4:30 to 6:30. What it meant was that diners could extend their eating until 6:30. Serving itself ended at 6:00.

At that moment, a book I had written during the pandemic, *The Kitchen is Closed: And Other Benefits of Being Old*, was being prepared for publication. I had closed my kitchen in Emeryville to arrive at one that was closed to me. The task, I firmly told my sinking self, was not to take this as any kind of omen—merely a disheartening coincidence.

Dinner will now commence promptly at 5:45, I told myself, carrying a small plastic bag containing a Styrofoam container with my rapidly cooling dinner as I reentered my disordered space. I hadn't considered what time I ate for decades. I ate when I was hungry, when meeting friends, or when using a phrase I love, when my mouth was lonely. This had been my abrupt and disheartening introduction to institutional living. I put on Rachel Maddow, propped the lukewarm crabcakes and coleslaw on my lap, and managed not to weep.

After a day of unpacking and creating a sense of order, I went down to dinner precisely at 5:45. Approaching a table where Malka, a woman with whom I had earlier exchanged a smile and a hello was holding forth, I quickly learned my second important lesson. Residents dine on time and choose the people they eat with.

She looked alarmed to see me settling myself on the chair beside her and turned confusedly towards her husband, who squared his spindly shoulders and said,

"I have bad news for you."

Has someone died? I thought. I don't know anyone here to feel bad about that. And that's almost always what bad news for old people means. His wife timidly entered the conversation.

"This is a set table of six. The same people always eat together."

"It's set in stone," her husband added.

"But we don't always have six," she added encouragingly, presumably letting me know I could sit with them if a regular died, got sick, or had other plans.

"I see," was the best I could manage as I rose from the table; the fourteen-year-old who had gone into the high school lunchroom at the start of the semester and unwittingly sat down at the table filled with what turned out to be the popular kids. Bobby Friedlander and Judy Hirschman looked at me and, unable to find words strong enough to communicate the egregiousness of my presence, simply stared until I got up to leave. I was an unpopular girl, and the awkward, ungainly, unpopular girls had their own table. I didn't belong. Their eye rolls were all that was needed then for me to absent myself—from their table and the entire lunchroom. Now, seventy years later, I left the dining room with the same mix of embarrassment, anger, and a strong desire to become invisible. So much for maturity.

The next morning, there was an insistent knock on my door. I opened it to a tall, rangy man whose face was nearly obscured by large dark glasses and a Let's Go Brandon ball cap, a euphemism encouraging viewers to Fuck Joe Biden, standing in my doorway after I answered his firm knock.

"I wanted to say welcome," he said.

Fuck Joe Biden? Was this guy a harbinger of the politics of the Desert Manor? Had I stumbled into a Trumpian haven of retired believers?

"Come in," I said politely. In what world would I have asked a man I didn't know, and on top of that, a man wearing a Let's Go Brandon cap into my apartment? Never. But here I was in this new life, and I didn't want to begin by revealing my worst qualities and behaving in a suspicious and judgmental way. Maybe by being someone else, someone I had always intended to become, a kind welcoming woman who would invite a strange man wearing a Let's Go Brandon cap would provide a better launch into Desert Manor.

He stumbled to my sofa and began to talk, perhaps assuming I was already seated nearby.

"I have macular degeneration," he said.

"Oh," I replied, racing for the next sentence. "That must be hard for you," the best I could come up with. The Let's Go Brandon cap had thrown me off my conversational game.

Mel had been a dentist before he had to close his practice, unable to see into his patients' mouths. He and his friends used to go to the gym every Thursday, to the track for the races, he went on, describing the life he had once led. Nothing about who he was now, which, given the aforementioned cap, was probably a wise decision.

I made oversized nods to be sure he could see I was there. When he asked me what I thought about his grandson calling him a racist because he didn't think the Redskins should have to change their name, he finished by letting me know the correct answer.

"Everyone is turning into snowflakes these days," he said.

As a proud dyed-in-the-wool snowflake, I answered with something purposefully vague like, "You know kids and their certainties," desperate to shift the conversation.

It didn't work. He went on to explain Trump's energy policy, even though the last thing in the world I would have encouraged was anything about the topic of Donald Trump.

"If only he had kept his fingers off all that Twitter business. His fossil fuel policies were good ones."

He didn't say, "Drill, baby, drill," but it's what he meant. When he finally rose to leave, his final bon mot was a wish for a Republican discussion group because he was surrounded by all these snowflake Democrats. I was relieved on two counts. First, I was, at least by his standards, living in a field of snowflakes, and second, I wouldn't have to interact with Mel again unless I was near enough for him to see me, and I'd make it my business to be sure that didn't happen.

Shirley, who lived directly across the hall, was next to introduce herself, although her doorway and the surrounding corridor walls covered with a Steinberg poster of Brooklyn, an illustrated 2022 calendar, a collage of family photos, and what appeared to be some kind of abstract image she had made in the art room had already given me a pretty clear visual introduction. She caught me returning from the trash chute at the far end of the hall and announced,

"I'm Shirley, your across-the-street neighbor."

"Hi, across-the-street Shirley," was the only answer that came to mind.

She walked alongside me until we reached my front door, which she pushed open, entering ahead of me.

Shirley was a sturdy bottle blonde woman wearing a tee shirt that displayed her love of New York and was further decorated with several bracelets, two rings, and bright lipstick that corresponded with her red toenails peeking out of sandals studded with glass jewels, all of which created an insistent fashion statement. She moved past me into the living room and said,

"So, you have the two bedrooms, right?"

She knew that I had the two bedrooms—she probably knew the people who had it before me. But before I could answer, she had settled into my armchair and begun her interrogation.

"How come you haven't come down to dinner? You've been here a couple of days already. You're not gonna meet anybody unless you do."

It appeared that Shirley was going to be the observer, the commenter, the telling-people-what-to-do neighbor.

"Well, it seems that everybody already has their table, and there's not much flexibility," I responded, angry at myself and at her for how defensive and pitiful I sounded.

"Well, that's true, but still, there are times people are away, or sick," she persisted.

She glanced around my living room, assessing my furniture, rugs, artwork, tchotchkes, and assorted throw pillows, and continued her questioning.

"Where did you move from?"

"The San Francisco Bay Area," I replied.

"How come you came to Phoenix?"

These were the opening salvos in the barrage of questions that followed. Why did I move? How many children did I have? Grandchildren?

Each of my answers led to the next question, making me feel like a convict sitting under a bright light trying to convince the police of her innocence. When she paused for breath, I said,

"How long have you been living here?" trying to turn the focus away from me and into something more like a conversation.

She explained that she had moved in two years ago because either her breathing or her blood pressure seemed to have been the final medical straw. I couldn't figure out which was at the root of her decline because she kept switching back and forth between lung and blood. Probably, they were somehow related. But perhaps she didn't understand how or why.

"My daughter is in charge of me now and takes me to all my doctor's appointments because she says I don't listen to what they tell me, and someone needs to keep track of what I'm supposed to do," she said. I already suspected that trying to be in charge of Shirley would be a thankless activity.

Eventually, she rose, and at my door, she turned back and said with the certainty and firmness I later learned characterized everything she said,

"My table is full, but if someone is sick or not coming down, I'll let you know, and you'll join us."

"Absolutely. Thanks."

But I whispered to the door closing behind her,

I'd rather eat a hardboiled egg standing over the sink than sit at your table.

After my inauspicious culinary beginnings, I picked up dinner in the café and ate upstairs for a few days, gathering up the psychological steam I'd need to try again. When I felt sufficiently emboldened, I went downstairs and moved towards a table that had some empty seats.

"May I join you?" I'd ask smilingly. If there was even a split second of confusion, I widened my smile which already felt like a rictus, and made my way to the exit. It was like musical chairs, but without the music and without the fun.

Twenty-five years before, I had moved my mother into a senior living residence much like Desert Manor, a residence she scornfully referred to as a "place."

"Promise me you'll never put me in a place when I'm old," she commanded after my father died. I promised, but after she could no longer hear and was unable to tolerate wearing hearing aids, and after she lost her license because she rear-ended a police car, after she was unable to go outside during the cold New England winters, after everything that had once constituted her life was out of reach, I broke my promise.

Her handwriting revealed her decline, letters with misspellings, lost words, and dropped phrases. During each of my visits, I found scraps of paper upon which she had written what she wanted to remember to tell me when we spoke on the phone and reminders of what she needed to do that day. She practiced writing her address, apartment number, state, and zip code on small pieces of paper as though she were giving herself an exam. Next to Mass., she wrote, state. Next to her address, she put the name of the condo building. Who were these answers for? What was she practicing? When my daughters were young, I taught them their addresses and phone numbers in case of an emergency. What emergencies did she fear?

I flew to Boston to move my mother across the country into the Reutlinger Center for Jewish Seniors, a place near me. Mealtimes there had staff assigned tables, thus avoiding in-groups barring residents from joining them. She was to sit with three lively and interesting women. I joined her for dinner for support and encouragement during those early weeks, but she was unable to hear their conversation. I saw how she put on her public smile and pretended to follow what was being said, hoping that her reply was relevant. But, eventually, the stress of getting dressed up to go down the dining room, which she understood as going out to dinner, straining to hear, combined with her increasing lack of appetite and lifelong social awkwardness, made mealtimes more stressful than had she remained on her sofa eating a microwaved sweet potato and wearing her comfortable in-the-house clothes.

Eventually, I began sneaking her food. Sneaking was necessary because residents were only permitted to have snacks in their tiny refrigerator, presumably intended to encourage them to gather in the dining room. I'd park around the back alongside the service vehicles, climb over the shrubbery, balancing my plastic bags filled with her groceries, and cross the gravel path to her back door. Her handwritten shopping list included:

- orange or tangerine juice
- small curd cottage cheese
- havarti with dill cheese
- instant coffee
- 1% milk
- rotisserie chicken cut up into quarters- (not Safeway it's no good)
- sweet potatoes
- Schweppes ginger ale (please open bottles for me)
- six-pack prune juice and v-8 juice
- jelly—without seeds
- bread—without seeds
- Corn Flakes
- Equal
- soups for microwave

I, too, had begun to shop and fill my kitchen cabinets to avoid the vulnerability of being turned away from the dining room that was to have fed me.

My list included:

- Fresh squeezed orange juice
- Peet's coffee
- Strawberry jelly
- Seeded rye bread
- Honeycrisp apples
- Manchego cheese
- Noosa lemon yogurt

Those items were augmented with mac and cheese, soups, and casseroles my daughters lovingly prepared to fill my freezer. I stole small containers of 2% milk, butter, Raisin Bran packets, sugar, and condiments from the dining room after nine at night when everything was closed and dark. I figured that was the least Desert Manor could do.

Both my mother and I ended up in a place, eating our dinners in drawstring pants, on the sofa, watching the news.

Nine
Playing Games

I had always considered games as something people played when there was nothing else to do. Once I learned to read, books always took precedence.

My mother played bridge, her sister played canasta and mahjong, and my brother played pool. I read books. I was a tall, awkward, shy and friendless girl, and my imagination didn't extend to the possibility that one day I would be, while still tall, not awkward, shy or friendless. But each week, the six books I took home from the library created imaginative possibilities for a less doomed future.

When my daughters were young, we played go fish, which I used to help them learn numbers and then gin after they'd mastered them. Candyland was their first board game, after which we graduated to Chinese and regular checkers. Monopoly was added to the mix when my daughters had outgrown Sorry and Clue, about which I have political regrets. My history with game playing is a very abbreviated one.

One morning, while I was accumulating my steps on the treadmill, a man sitting in a nearby chair began a conversation by asking if I had been raised on a farm, which I understood to mean that he was commenting on my steady stride. He added, "You seem in pretty good shape. Do you mind if I ask how old you are?"

When I replied that I was eighty-three, he then assertively stated that he was nearly ninety and displayed his youthful vigor by lifting the two-pound weights to his shoulders three times.

Elmo played checkers and chess and kept his equipment with him as he glided through the building on his scooter, always ready in case someone wanted to play. He stationed himself at the table by the doorway, which allowed him to see everyone going in and out of the main gathering area. Whenever a resident passed, he looked up, made eye contact, and lifted his eyebrows with a question and invitation.

After several such silent invitations, I sat down to play. I hadn't played in more than fifty years, but how complicated could it be? It was just checkers.

I also imagined it a kindness to play with this old man who was so eager for a partner but was immediately disavowed of my assumption after losing to his triple jump. How could that be? I'd try again. I did. After five games, I shamefacedly acknowledged that Elmo was a master checkers player and, luckily for me, one who enjoyed teaching.

I leaned back in my chair and said,

"Well, if we're going to play together. You're going to have to teach me how to beat you."

He smiled and explained,

"There are only four moves in checkers. If you're not positioned where you want to be, you've lost the game."

I had no idea what that meant, but knew I would learn if I played with him. And I did at every chance I got. I never won, but got better at seeing at least two moves ahead. Still, every game concluded with his triumphant double, or even more humiliatingly, triple jump. He always praised me, saying I was one of his few challengers in the community, which I hoped was true because I wanted to beat this kind. potbellied suspender-wearing farmer. Just once.

Bingo, which was the most popular activity at Desert Manor by far, required hoping your winning number would get called. That was it. Taking a chance on the randomness of numbers didn't involve any skill, although I could see and appreciate the camaraderie of women enjoying the easy and offhand social interactions they shared while waiting for the drama of each wheel spin, the eager anticipation of a moment of chance.

I once had a lover who took me to Las Vegas. He was drawn to roulette and blackjack, which he tried repeatedly to explain to me—both how they worked and why they were so exhilarating. He could have been describing what was under the hood of my car, as other men had tried to do, to absolutely no avail. I busied myself at the slot machines while he played his games, and aside from strengthening whatever muscle it is that you use when pulling the lever down repeatedly, nothing happened. Not even a little bunch of quarters. I'm simply not a winner in the waiting-for-a-number department. Our love affair ended soon thereafter as well.

My problem was that nearly everyone played bingo; only Elmo played checkers, and I had to wait for the staff to be free to play ping-pong. So, if I were to meet people and make friends, games weren't going to get me there. I was going to have to find another way to become a part of Desert Manor's social life.

Ten
As a Lesbian, I Don't Like These Crab Cakes

I quickly learned that Mel of the Let's Go Brandon ball cap carried a flask of vodka with him. He fell repeatedly in his efforts to return to his apartment after his secret imbibing—which, of course, was no longer a secret after all those falls.

Being around drinkers was hard for me, even after being sober for twenty-five years. I could still recognize myself in every slurred word, every repetition, and every overly dramatic insistence. Alcohol allowed me to identify what I was angry about or afraid of without the need to do anything to change. My observations during my drinking years were rich and deep and complex, but just the right number of gin and tonics allowed them to remain astonishing, oft-repeated insights.

But as my sixtieth birthday approached and I faced the history of both my father's and my brother's alcoholism, as well as my own decades of repeated and failed attempts at reaching something that resembled moderation, I knew it was time for me to stop. As Anne Lamott so sagely defined that moment, it's when we wake up "in pitiful and degraded enough shape to take Step Zero, which is: 'This shit has got to stop.'"

And stop I did, substituting cold Fresca in a chilled wine glass every day at 5:00 for several months. The years since that chastening and necessary decision have been some of the best and clearest of my life.

Everyone at Desert Manor apparently gave Mel's drinking and falling down a pass because he was seen as connected because his son Aaron, was the activities director. But within two weeks of my arrival, an evening when I happened to be eating at a nearby table, he apparently said something derogatory about Jill Biden, a woman Shirley revered both as a teacher and the woman who saved Joe Biden from tremendous suffering after the death of his wife and daughter in an automobile accident, helping to raise his two remaining children.

These were central values for her, and she rose to her feet and did what my grandmother called "opening up a mouth."

"His wife and child died," she began, at top volume. "How can you say anything bad about a woman who gave him another chance at life?"

Shirley did righteous hollering like a pro, and she let him have it. Without waiting to see what came next, she reached for her walker and stalked out, leaving Mel bewildered and his entire table shocked into uncharacteristic silence. The dining room quieted for a few minutes until the eager whispers began, each table parsing out the explosion to suit their own perspective of Shirley, of Mel, of Jill Biden, and of proper dining room behavior.

Shirley had her table, and Malka and Benny had theirs, places where I would be welcome if someone was sick, dead, or away. Neither was a compelling set of choices. Of course, there were other tables, but nearly all of them were full, and rather than return to the disheartening obstacle course of trying to find a spot to sit down, I decided to skip dinner and have lunch as my second meal. I could always pull something together and watch the news, which had been my usual culinary MO at dinnertime for years. Pulling something together.

Breakfast, served in the café, consisted of oatmeal, scrambled eggs, bacon, and sausages presented in steam trays, along with assorted individual portions of Special K, Raisin Bran, and Wheaties, small containers of milk, bananas, and apples, and coffee, all served by young women in hairnets and plastic gloves. The scene was reminiscent of my high school cafeteria filled with chattering teenagers sliding their trays forward for a main course we identified as mystery meat. We'd fill our trays and disperse to the tables that defined our assigned categories—nerds, popular, athletes, artists, and assorted leftovers. I was a leftover in high school.

Now I was in another cafeteria, this one without a long line because residents couldn't stand for very long. There were chairs carefully arranged in front of the steam tables so residents could rest while waiting their turn at the buffet. I had come all this way to be back at the beginning—another cafeteria—another leftover.

Now, after skipping dinner, I decided to forgo breakfast as well, and have Special K and bananas in my apartment. It wasn't just the hairnets and gloves that put me off, although they felt discomfortingly gynecologic. It was the steam trays. I wasn't expecting olive oil-infused orange pound cake or an everything bagel with mascarpone and capers. It was the idea of being served—again—by all those gloved hands.

That left lunch. I had to eat something, somewhere, otherwise, what was the point of even being at Desert Manor? I didn't choose the dining room, which was open for business, but went to the café at noon, confident I would be able to sit down without fear of being rebuffed. Since residents either went into the dining room or had lunch in their apartments, it was rarely full. I took a book along with me so it would appear I was doing something, but something that might be interruptible if an approaching resident was so inclined. Lunch, like breakfast and dinner, was served from the ever-present steam trays in Styrofoam containers, with the side dishes to the fish or chicken offered up in perfect scoops.

I staked out a spot at the back table by the door leading out to the pool. That way I was able to face the dance floor/performance space and see everything that was going on. Across the room and against the far wall was a woman similarly situated, always sitting in the same chair, always crocheting. We were the sentinels observing the daily life of Desert Manor reveal itself between our posts.

I approached her to introduce myself, and in our brief conversation, she let me know that she wasn't a "joiner," didn't like planned activities, was a devout Christian, and liked to watch more than participate. Each of these identifiers was stated in a clear, no-nonsense voice. Finishing her explanation, she reached into the straw basket beside her and thrust what appeared to be a red, white, and blue crocheted potholder into my hand, a clear gesture indicating the end of any further interaction. I had been dismissed and took my patriotic potholder across the room and, with my back to her, tossed it into a trash container. I didn't want a fucking potholder. I wanted someone to talk to me.

After several days of eating mediocre food while trying to maintain an interested and engaged expression on my face in case anyone wanted to approach me, a woman carrying a tray of macaroni and cheese asked if she could join me. Join me? *Are you kidding?* I thought. That's why I'm sitting here by myself. Hoping.

She moved with an awkward gait, and it was clear that something was the matter with her legs. Lowering herself carefully into a chair, she apologetically began by telling me that she had two bum knees that she wasn't planning to replace, having heard too many accounts of failed surgeries.

"I'll just climb into a wheelchair when I can't get around anymore," she said.

But knee surgery is just fancy carpentry, I thought. It seemed a fearful way to age. But what was it my business? Marion turned out to be an interesting companion. She'd been a political worker in the Democratic party after retiring as a child probation officer for juvenile offenders and had an encyclopedic knowledge of politics in Maricopa County, the largest and currently most contentious political entity in Arizona. She even offered a discussion group called Politics once a month in the Cinema Room. *Now we're talking,* I thought. This woman knew so much about what I wanted to learn. Forget the knees. Maybe we could figure out some kind of political activism together. It was, after all, Arizona, a state sorely in need of everything in the activism department.

Marion talked at devoted length about her father who had been a Marxist describing him as her most significant political mentor. She'd tried to model her life after his as much as she could, although she confessed she wasn't as much of a go-getter as he had been, a fact I had already intuited from her decision about her knees.

Eventually, other residents joined me at my lunchtime perch, even groups of them, but mostly to continue whatever conversation they were already having.

After a few obligatory welcomes and where are you from, talk turned to the quality of the meals (almost always critical, leading into a lengthy conversation about how to correctly prepare said dish), the entertainment (usually enthusiastic if it involved singing or dancing), and their bodies—in unapologetic granular detail.

Lillian had lost a front tooth after a fall but couldn't have a substitute implanted because she'd had a stroke and the medications she took precluded surgery. This visible absence was a source of embarrassment for her, and she was always full of apologies. Her missing a tooth wasn't a problem for me. It was the fact that she self-consciously covered her mouth when she spoke which meant I couldn't hear her and had to guess what she was saying. Florence had a hammer toe, Brenda was deciding whether to change her blood pressure medication, and Ellen needed a bypass.

Once, I had been impatient with these organ recitals. I waited for the stories about this illness and that doctor to finish so we could move on to what I hoped would be a more engaging conversation. But I understood the signals better now and knew no one lived here because they wanted to but because they were out of choices. They came because they forgot the right things and remembered the wrong ones. They came because, after the third dinged fender, their children insisted they stop driving. They came because they couldn't keep track of their daily vitamins and medicines. They came because they couldn't climb the stairs, handle the winter, or remember the names of their grandchildren. They came because they needed to relinquish their autonomy for an institutional form of independence. Identifying what parts of their bodies weren't working well—or at all—was their way of explaining why they were living at Desert Manor and no longer in their own homes.

There was always at least a mention of the children and the grandchildren. They shared photos accompanied by proud descriptions of said offspring's accomplishments in grade school, college, or work. Everyone assumed that I had grandchildren. The fact of their existence was a given. When I explained I didn't have any, their faces shifted from surprise to curiosity, then to pity. I would quickly begin to talk about Evan, who was then fifteen, describing his terrificness to their still sorry-for-me faces. But godchildren weren't the same as grandchildren. I was found lacking in the lineage department.

I was lacking in the heterosexual department, too. My simple declarative sentence identifying myself as a lesbian in a conversation with Marion elicited a simple nod; my nonheterosexuality left me in an awkward and unfamiliar closet. There were no other lesbians at Desert Manor. Not a single one. There were a few men who described themselves as roommates, and while I didn't know who they thought they were fooling, clearly, they needed to try. Undoubtedly, some children and grandchildren were somewhere on the LGBTQ+ continuum, but if there were, they weren't mentioned, until one afternoon when Shirley, who often talked about her disappointment that her daughters didn't get along, inadvertently used a pronoun that revealed her eldest's sapphic-ness. I pounced on it.

"Is Barbara a lesbian?" I asked in a mild voice to cover my eagerness.

"She is and has been since she was in junior high. All the sports and athletic this and that, I should have known then," Shirley said.

"Is that why your girls don't get along?" I persisted.

"Well, only partly. There's a whole lot more," she said, crossing her arms over her chest, signaling that part of the conversation was over.

But I had one more sentence to add.

"I'm a lesbian, Shirley. Your across-the-street friend is a lesbian."

"That's nice, dear," was her firm reply.

The subject was never mentioned again.

I would have to find a way to work my lesbian self into a conversation and not make an announcement. So far, that opportunity hadn't arisen. What were the options? I couldn't say,

"As a lesbian, I don't like these crab cakes."

I imagined the residents I met probably thought that lesbians were people who had sex with one another, and since it didn't appear that anyone at Desert Manor, except the staff, was having sex, how and with whom we used to have sex no longer seemed a category of relevance. But this was who I was, and who I'd been for fifty years. Sex came and went, but being a lesbian remained. Given Shirley's evident reticence about her daughter's identity, I suspected my coming out to her wouldn't be shared with the wider community. And it wasn't.

Marion and I became regulars at lunch a couple of times a week, during which I ate salads, thereby avoiding the steam trays, while I absorbed the history of precinct-level machine politics, gerrymandering designed to carve out new red districts, and the history of the judges who sailed unchallenged from one election to the next. This seemed promising. There were voter registration projects to create. Candidates to vet. Plus, I enjoyed our time together. Her struggles to walk put a damper on some of my more extravagant plans, but I was so relieved to have a political companion, that I figured I'd find a way to finesse her physical limitations. I still drove, after all.

Eleven
Driving All the Miss Daisys

"You drive, right?" Shirley asked.

"I do," I answered hesitantly, already fearing what was coming next.

"The next time you're going out, can I get a lift to the corner? It'll only take a second. I have to run into the market and get some cottage cheese."

The corner nearest Desert Manor was two city blocks of box stores called Valley Plaza Mall. There was a Target, a Walmart, and a Home Depot, but nothing resembling a market. There was never parking, always crowds, rarely anyone masked, and there was no one at Desert Manor who was able to run anywhere. Those days were long gone.

Of course, I said yes. As someone who still drove, surrounded by so many who no longer did, I had to say yes. I couldn't say I was busy because it was clear I wasn't. No one at Desert Manor was busy. I had had one chance to lie, and I didn't take it. Once I said I drove, my goose was all the way cooked.

When I was a young woman, I finally said yes to going all the way with my boyfriend. What I hadn't understood with that yes, was that he (it was he then), assumed that since we had already had sex, we would then end every date by having sex. No further asking was required. We only got one yes. I had given my one yes to Shirley.

On our second trip to the deli across town, Shirley told me how she had orchestrated a community-wide campaign against an outsider who introduced himself to Gladys, the unsuspecting daily scheduler, as a Jew for Jesus, and offered to provide a Purim celebration. Gladys, always looking for opportunities to beef up her programming, had appreciatively accepted.

When Shirley got wind of it, knowing that Jews for Jesus were not Jews at all, but Christians who believed that Jesus was the son of God, the true Messiah, and tried to convert Jews to Christianity, she took it upon herself to put an end to such dangerous attempts at propaganda.

"What kind of business is this to OK a Jew for Jesus here? Plus, Gladys doesn't know a thing about Jews She ought to be trained to do her job properly. I'm going to Aaron."

He was the staff member who made sure that things ran smoothly. For Shirley, men in authority solved problems. But just to cover her bases, she consulted with the Chabad rabbi, whose congregants were the Jews in all the senior facilities scattered throughout the city. He urged her to put a stop to such nonsense, and his agreement and support fueled this affront to her Jewish self.

She carried the rabbi's concern to Aaron, one male voice speaking to the other with Shirley as the courier. The outcome was that Purim was, as it always had been, a dress-up affair held at the Scottsdale Jewish Center.

She repeatedly regaled me with detailed accounts, each centrally organized around how, had it not been for her, catastrophes would have befallen her children, her husband, the company she worked for, her temple, or her friends. She was certain about the correct way to do everything and voluble in her expression of outrage when people had other ways. She was there to set things right if they were, in her mind, even mildly improper. And she was just across the hall.

Occasionally, we'd sit on her balcony, one that was on the opposite side of the building and consequently less attractive to the pigeons, drink generic frozen lemonade mix, and visit. Her apartment was filled with glass cabinets stuffed with pictures of children and grandchildren, graduation photos, wedding pictures, figurines, and random objects that clearly had personal historic resonance. Every surface was littered with objects, even scattered over the small table where she ate her breakfast. Her living room was an insistent announcement of her past. Every graduation, wedding, birth, and vacation was displayed. This is what my life has been. This is who I am and what I want you to know.

My living room was very unlike hers. It was purposefully spare, and except for a few photos on the refrigerator, there were none of my family. All those images were in the back bedroom which served as my office. They were not for display. All my apartments had been arranged in that way. My past did not insist upon itself when people entered my living room. It was in the past, where it belonged.

I could have put my wedding pictures with Barbara on the coffee table, or hung posters of me at demonstrations, holding signs or giving speeches. I could have even designed a living room like Norman Mailer's self-congratulatory book, *Advertisements for Myself*. But I didn't want to. I wanted them to ask me about myself because they were interested, as I did when meeting them.

One afternoon, while drinking Shirley's execrable lemonade, I told her about my ex-husband Wally, now living in a residential facility nearby and about to turn ninety-eight. He and I had eventually settled into an easy companionability after a painful divorce nearly sixty years before, and I told her how comforted I was to have both him and my daughters nearby.

"Our original family has come back into a kind of alignment. There have been other wives, other lovers, but now, at the end of both of our lives, we're back in connection again."

"Well, long relationships don't always end that happily," she began, warming up to a story, and by the way she shifted her position and leaned forward to be sure I was paying attention, I could already tell it was going to be an aggrieved one.

It centered on a falling out with Sylvia, a woman who had been a close friend of more than forty years. The two women raised their children together, and the couple went on holiday every year until Sylvia and her husband moved across the country. After some financial reversals, she could no longer afford the airfare, so Shirley's husband sent them money for travel, and they continued their relationship in that financially asymmetrical way for decades. She paused and put her hand on my arm to be sure I didn't miss a single bit of this next part.

"When Benny died, Sylvia called to express her sympathies and asked if she should come to the funeral. Can you believe she asked me a question like that? What was she thinking? Was I supposed to tell her to come from Florida to say goodbye to a man who she had known for forty years, who was so good to her, who gave her money when she needed it? I couldn't believe it," Shirley exploded.

She paused and looked sternly at me. It was clear how I was supposed to respond. That Sylvia might have felt ashamed to ask for the plane fare or thought that coming after the shiva period had ended so the two of them might be together wasn't part of Shirley's wounded calculus.

"I haven't talked to her since that phone call," she announced.

Her decision was final. And permanent.

As a young newlywed, I had witnessed that meticulous scorekeeping after becoming part of my husband's extended tribe. Family gatherings were enormous, and Pearl, a middle-aged unmarried woman was responsible for keeping track of all the birthdays, anniversaries, and occasional deaths in the cousin's club, which included all the husbands, wives, and children. It was a demanding task, and she was proud of her role in the family. But the most important and delicate part of her job was being in charge of the table arrangements at all family events. She was the one who knew why the Denver cousins could never, under any circumstances, be seated at the same table as the Wisconsin cousins. All that was required was one sentence to the hostess.

"You can't put them together. They don't talk."

The Denver and Wisconsin cousins might no longer remember why that mandate needed to be honored. Perhaps it was something to do with what a father-in-law had said or done or what an aunt had forgotten to say or do decades earlier.

Whatever it was, the slight continued to be completely unforgivable. Forever.

Pearl made sure that succeeding generations would never be caught at the table of someone on the other side of the insult, even if no one remembered what said insult was. An angry interaction or bad business decision could end any connection to an entire branch of one's family. She was the keeper of the flame, and the urgencies of loyalty and betrayal continued to burn hot within her unmarried heart.

I had seen women similarly exile one another during my early feminist days. Both the very real and imagined differences between liberal feminists, political feminists, cultural feminists, lesbian feminists, separatist feminists, and anti-racist feminists were sufficient to lay waste to fields of eager revolutionary beginners.

But Shirley was not someone with whom I wanted to get into all of that, the wounds caused, the prices paid, so chickenshit that I was after she finished, I murmured,

"That sounds like it was a painful rupture."

"Painful for me. That was it. Can you believe such a thing?"

"Wow," was the best I could manage. Asking for another glass of lemonade managed to turn the conversation to the pros and cons of frozen or canned lemonade, a considerably less fraught subject leaving Shirley's outrage for another day. And I knew there would be another day and other outrages—many of them.

Rosalyn often joined us on what Shirley called her "errands," since she was always looking for an opportunity to get a manicure. She had lost her driver's license because she was losing her memory and was increasingly unable to find her way home. Before moving to Phoenix, she had been active in her temple sisterhood in Chicago and raised twins, one very successful about whom she spoke at great length and the other who had died and was seldom mentioned.

Israel and the temple sisterhood were at the center of Rosalyn's life. She counted on Shirley to remind her where to be for activities and meals, but once there, she became a bottomless well of detailed memories about her growing up, her early years at the synagogue, her friendship circles, and her "balabusta years." She was proud of her history. And of her nails, wearing multiple rings to decorate what she felt remained of her good looks. Rosalyn did indeed have beautiful hands and had manicures as often as I would take her to the salon.

Like my boyfriend of old, she didn't ask after the first yes— just lifted her eyebrows expressively and questioningly when she saw me. My job was to interpret her face and let her know when I was next going in the neighborhood of her salon.

Within weeks, I was widely identified as someone who drove. I began to enter and leave the building through the back entrance to avoid being stopped and asked for a ride. Someone always had either a doctor's appointment at 3:40 the next day, or needed to go to the grocery store, but a specific store across town because their prices were better, and it was cleaner than the markets that were closer. I didn't feel good about myself as I ducked as many of those requests as I could, but feeling mild to moderately bad about myself was a price I was willing to pay.

This was not working out as I had imagined. I wasn't being fed by friendly waitstaff in a dining room overlooking the rolling green expanse of lawn. I was eating take-out from the deli department of Whole Foods in my apartment or out of Styrofoam in the café. I wasn't making friends. I was sneaking around, trying to avoid everybody. I didn't play pool or bingo. I didn't make art projects that echoed the lanyards and macaroni necklaces my children had made in camp. I was willing to try harder but didn't know what trying harder would look like.

Twelve
Esther Williams Redux

My relationship with the other residents was not unfolding as I had hoped, but I continued to maintain my efforts to keep my body strong and as supple as my 84 years would permit. Every morning, I went down to the pool to do what I still identified as swimming. The primary drawback was that I could no longer swim. I do things that, if you're not looking closely, might resemble swimming. Doing the forward crawl, moving your face from side to side while breathing in unison with the strokes, well, that's over.

I have an arthritic shoulder which meant the end of crawling. I could, however, do a mean side stroke. On one side, anyway. My legs continued to be strong, so I made bicycle circles, kicking and enjoying the lower half of my body. Now that real swimming is no longer an athletic possibility, I've renamed what I do as water yoga. My practice on land in recent years has been intermittent, but my ability to hold dramatic stances like the warrior pose while in the water is dazzling. Of course, there are no longer sun salutations or anything involving an inversion since I'm standing in the pool. It's also the case that I was never good at inversions under the best of much younger circumstances.

After gliding up and back in my creatively designed forms of movement, I moved to the edge of the pool for my morning yoga. I began with leg swings, placing my right hand lightly, very lightly on the side, imagining I was a ballerina—an old lesbian ballerina.

I lifted my leg until my toes peeked out of the water, then slowly, deliberately, and hopefully gracefully swung my leg back behind me, holding each movement for an ever-increasing count. I managed twenty-five seconds on each end of the lift, doing a couple dozen of those. Then I swung off to the side for another couple of dozen reps—reps being a word people who exercise use.

Then, I moved on to the more demanding parts of my watery practice. Lifting my arm, I intended to make a smooth and perhaps even sinuous arc as I bent to the side. My left side managed a mediocre arc, but the other resulted in a grunt, which I tried to keep as quiet as possible in case anyone was listening or watching, which no one was. They were in the café having breakfast and visiting.

The side stretch was all I could manage for my upper body since my shoulder hurt if I moved it around it too much. I concluded my practice with several underwater lunges that were Balanchine-ian and a tree pose that, with some waving of my arms to keep balance, felt athletic.

While I was working to keep myself in the best Esther Williams-ish shape I could, and maybe even imagining some improvement, I was also having to attend to the body I currently had. This required navigating the medical establishment with the constellation of preexisting conditions that invariably accompany oldness. I had to create a medical safety net for my body, every part of which had its own specialist. Eyes, ears, teeth, skin, lungs, heart, and kidneys required specific attention. None of those doctors talked to each other, although they would each talk to me. I created a spreadsheet to keep track of everybody.

Each required waits of several months before I could get into their overflowing practices, and I was left to hope that the relevant part of my body wouldn't need medical attention before then. Maintenance now involved medications, supplements, sunscreen, and inhalers, all of which augmented the time when I began my day by merely brushing my teeth. My hair was thinning, my hips were thickening, my eyes were dimming, and my teeth appeared to be shifting. There was no cute part left anywhere on my body. So, I compensated by having pedicures. Not that old women's feet are cute. They're not. But something about having colorful toes felt youthful and insouciant in the face of the slippage that was occurring everywhere else.

I kept reminding myself, that my kids can't know how lost I felt, even though the kids in question were well into their sixties. Who was I protecting? And from what?

Thirteen
Praying at Desert Manor

I'd often return to the café in the late afternoon for a Sprite and to see who was around, since by then there was no danger of anyone wanting a ride. There was always a rush into the dining room at 4:30 for the super early birds, but traffic slowed till 5:30 when the rest of the diners began to congregate.

During a late afternoon lull, Malka approached my table and asked if she could join me.

"Please," I replied, arranging my face into what I hoped resembled a welcoming smile.

She began to speak almost before her behind hit the chair, clearly anxious about whatever it was she had to say.

"I noticed you don't come into the dining room anymore and hoped it wasn't because I said you couldn't sit at our table."

"Well, it did seem a little bit inhospitable, given that I had just moved in," I couldn't resist saying.

"It's just that there are three couples and me and Benny planned it so carefully. There's Mel and Rachel, Ada and Jerry and us. Everybody does their tables like that. You figure out who you want to have your meals with, so you don't have to leave things to chance," she said, her voice trailing off as she heard herself. "But whenever anyone is on vacation, or sick..." she finished hopefully.

"I understand," I said with a firm voice, needing to put an end to this part of the conversation. Three couples? With the percentage of men and women at the Desert Manor approaching 20/80, she had orchestrated a grouping designed to reflect what life had looked like before all the men died.

Furthermore, having dinner with Mel while he sipped from his not-so-secret flask was the last thing in the world I'd want to do. Rachel had forgotten so much of who she was that all that remained was a warm vagueness. Ada and Jerry loved to display their recent joint efforts from art class and were always inviting people to try to beat them at ping pong, followed by a knowing chuckle. I couldn't imagine witty, intellectual wordplay at their dinner table. Listening to Rachel Maddow tell me an historically embedded analysis of the news would be better, more compelling company. Hands down.

I changed the subject by asking Malka why she moved to Desert Manor and became a central presence in the Jewish life here. She began further back than I had expected, almost at the beginning, explaining that something had gone wrong with her body when she was nineteen, about which she was either purposefully vague or medically unclear. Whatever it was resulted in her infertility, and she and Benny adopted a special needs child, which she felt was the Jewish thing to do. This now adult daughter was married to a man she scornfully described as a "rotten bum" who didn't want to work. The family had moved to Albania because it was the only country they could afford to live with their three children without someone, anyone, making a living. The rotten bum was also apparently unhealthy, and Malka hoped he would die so their daughter and grandchildren would have to return to the United States.

When they moved into Desert Manor, Norman had managed Jewish life. Everyone loved him, and after he died, she wanted to honor him by continuing what he had created, even though she knew she wasn't as well-liked as he had been.

"There was no one else to do it," she said. "So, it was the right thing to do."

It was becoming clear that Malka found a Jewish reason to do what she wanted, including adoption and creating a public role in this community. She was an old woman with failing health trying to do the right thing—honoring Norman, trying to live a good, responsible spiritual life, the exception being her wish for the death of her son-in-law. But didn't I want the same thing? To find where I fit and could be of use in this unfamiliar culture? And hadn't I wished for the death of people who had wounded me? Deaths that they understood as they were dying were directly caused by the ways they had hurt me. Of course, I had. Impulsively, I reached over and took her hand.

"How lucky we are to have you," I said.

Her eyes glistened and she turned away, pretending to reach for something in her canvas bag. The moment passed as Benny approached us and brusquely nodded in my direction. She stood, took his arm, and they moved towards the dining room and their table of six.

I finished my Sprite and went upstairs to pull something together. Tonight's repast would consist of the remaining half of the quiche Janaea had brought me, along with some sliced tomatoes. And, of course, rum raisin ice cream while I watched Rachel.

I was curious about the Shabbat services Benny and Malka led. While I was surprised they were held on Friday at 11:00 a.m., I told myself I could be theologically flexible. One month of Fridays later, I was ready to join whatever this would be and made my way to the Cinema Room, a dark, windowless space with rows of bulky leather-covered oversized chairs facing a massive blank screen. The walls were covered in movie posters that spanned the history of the medium. Rudolph Valentino looking lascivious, Rita Hayworth being tempestuous, Cary Grant, as always, debonair, and John Wayne permanently manly.

Malka stood by the door, greeting each attendee and handing them a Xeroxed prayer book. She welcomed me and seemed relieved that I had come. I sat down next to Rosalyn and near Benny, who was already in his seat next to the blank movie screen, with a computer on his lap. She walked over to a pair of electric candles on the ledge beneath the screen and coughed, which appeared to be the signal to quiet down.

The rules handbook I had been given the day I arrived made it clear that no fire of any kind was allowed at Desert Manor. No Shabbat candles in our apartments. No menorahs. No nothing. The combination of our oldness, their insurance premiums, and the ever-present possibility of a conflagration unwittingly begun by an inattentive resident required strict adherence to the need for alternative illumination.

Malka turned the electric bulbs on and led us in the blessing that began the service. Then Benny, at his wife's direction, which consisted of a brief eye command (they've been married for fifty-one years), pressed a button on his computer. An all-male Israeli chorus filled the screen, enthusiastically singing "Lecha Dodi" and inviting us to welcome the Sabbath. Several residents sang along; a man sitting in the back row wearing a yarmulke, the most animated of our elderly flock. We then moved on to the central prayer of the S'hma, as he continued his vigorous participation.

When the service moved to the prayer offering comfort and healing to the sick, Malka invited us to call out the names of those who needed healing. Nearly everyone had someone they wanted to include. Benny clicked again, and Debbie Freedman filled the screen singing Mi Shiberach, the blessing for healing. When Kaddish, the prayer to honor the dead was read, she again asked us to identify the names of those who had died. It seemed that providing an opportunity for residents to gather and call up the names of their sick and their dead was a central and comforting objective of the Shabbat morning service. After Adon Olam, the traditional triumphant closing hymn sung by another Israeli group on the big screen, Rosalyn passed around challah, wine, and grape juice as Malka led us in the blessings that accompanied each one. All of this was managed in an hour so that everyone could get to the dining room.

I found it unexpectedly comforting to be a part of an in-person gathering, even a one-hour-in-the-morning one after a congregational life that had existed entirely on Zoom during and since COVID. I had attended Friday night services, bought fresh flowers, lit candles, turned off my phone, and kept my attention on the screen, my electronic conduit to the divine. Now, my prayer life would be augmented with weekly expressions of reverence in the Cinema Room at Desert Manor on Friday before lunch. I'd make it work.

Fourteen
Jews Schmooze

Malka's second offering to the community was held on the following Wednesday. Originally, Norman had named the gathering the Yiddish Club, but because so many residents assumed that meant it was either a class in Yiddish or feared one had to be able to speak Yiddish to participate, it wasn't much of a success. After many meetings and much conversation, the name was changed to Jews Schmooze.

I took the elevator down to attend the meeting, imagining there would be a lively conversation about something. After all, what do old Jews do at a schmooze? They talk. They argue. They reminisce. I was looking forward to this.

As I walked down the hall that led to the Cinema Room, I saw that all the lights were out and worried I had gotten the date or hour wrong. But as I drew closer and asked Lillian, who was tooling past me in her scooter, if the Club was meeting, she enthusiastically said that everyone was looking forward to watching *Exodus*, Part One, chosen expressly by Benny.

Going to the movies in the middle of the afternoon to watch a forgettable film I had already seen decades before wasn't what I had hoped for from a schmooze. I wanted the schmoozing part. The being in a Club part.

"Thanks, Lil. I'll just go and get my glasses then," was the only excuse that came to mind as I turned to go. I hoped she didn't notice I was already wearing them.

I returned to my balcony, prudently enclosed with plastic spikes glued to the balcony railing to keep out the relentless pigeons. While my efforts had been successful, and my outdoor table and chair were no longer covered in pigeon shit, the spikes left me feeling enclosed, not like a princess in a tower waiting to drape my long hair out the window for the prince (or, in my case, princess) to ascend and save me, but like an old lady held prisoner in an alien universe.

I had come to Desert Manor to live among old Jews, but I arrived hauling a long, complicated history of Jewishness. I was a moderately knowledgeable practicing Jew, a lesbian-feminist Jew, and an activist Jew. But it appeared I had stumbled into a recreation of the conventional Jewish life I'd fled nearly fifty years before.

Benny's movie choices, shown on alternating Wednesdays, were all Jewishly themed, featuring Mel Brooks and Billy Crystal, alternating with documentaries that marked the triumphs of Jewish artists, scientists and writers. And everything about Israel. By now, I knew most of the Jewish residents by name. There was Shirley and Mel, Shana the artist, Norma who didn't speak to Shirley but loved to argue with Irene and everybody else she could corral, Dolly who was raised Orthodox and hated everything about her traditional upbringing, but always showed up for services, Ada and Jerry and Rosalyn, Shirley's sidekick.

There was Evie and Edie, or Edie and Evie, who always sat together at services and whispered. But only to each other. I had met one of them, although it was unclear to me which one. They were both small, with short dark hair; one had a soft face, and the other talked very fast, but those distinctions weren't enough for me to remember who was who. Evie or Edie seemed friendly and offered me her bottle of bubble gum pink nail polish after I had complimented her on the color, reaching for something to say in the awkwardly long pause after hello.

Kippah-wearing Dov always sat alone in the back row during Shabbat service and the Jews Schmooze meetings and rarely spoke, but when he did, it was to describe his escape from Russia when he was five. He told us about the border crossings, the Russian army, the Polish peasants who helped, and those who didn't. This was Dov's origin story. Malka always allowed him as much time to speak as he needed, even if he was disrupting something else she might have planned. He represented the Jewish story. Escaping. Fleeing. Starting over.

At the start of a Friday morning Shabbat service, he expressed concern that since there were only eight of us, we wouldn't be able to hold services because we didn't have ten worshippers, the required number for a minyan. Traditional practices, as they have been observed for centuries, comforted Dov. Even the denominations of Conservative and Reform seemed to him like a scattering of the tribes that, combined with the increase of intermarriage, left him fearful about the future of the Jewish people. He wasn't comforted by Malka assuring him our numbers didn't matter—it was our intention to join together in prayer that mattered. But he sighed, leaned back in his chair, and offered each prayer and song as loudly as he could. Perhaps he thought he had to make up for the missing congregants.

Within months, the number of attendees at the non-movie Wednesdays was down to the six or seven people who predictably filled the Cinema Room. When I asked Dolly, widely admired because she remembered the names of all the leading men and women (then called ladies) from every movie made in the 1940s, why there was such low attendance, she explained it was because "Malka was losing it."

This view was echoed by other women in the Quarter. I heard gossip circulating about her forgetting what she was talking about, wandering into a new topic with no advanced warning, coupled with her increasing difficulty hearing, held together by a stubborn self-protectiveness designed to manage her decline.

Shabbat prayers have a consistent order, so Malka was able to navigate the familiarity of the service successfully, but the schmooze was becoming either unruly or too small because the residents who came, because, like me, they wanted to be around other Jews for a couple of hours a week, either dozed off, couldn't hear, or weren't interested in the conversation Malka was trying to create. First challah and then wine disappeared from the traditional ending of the service, Sam no longer wanting to pick them up. Then he forgot to order movies from the library, so schmoozing got canceled. Desert Manor's organized Jewish life appeared to be deteriorating.

Fifteen
A Vilde Chaya

The following Friday morning before services began and while everyone was getting settled, Malka asked how many people defined themselves as Conservative and how many as Reform. After all the raised hands were counted, I took a deep breath, waved my arm around to get her attention, and said that I was a Renewal Jew.

She paused, looked confused, and then gave me the smile she gave everyone who spoke, the one that unequivocally delighted in whatever had been said. At the end of services, she approached me to ask if I would talk about whatever Renewal was at the next Jews Schmooze.

"I'd be happy to," I said, hoping that might provide the opportunity for me to come out as an activist, spiritual, lesbian Jew.

I expected the seven or eight people who always showed up, but perhaps because people were curious about me, or possibly because Malka had talked about this unexpected development at dinner, nearly twenty-five residents came.

Malka took charge, fluttering around, welcoming everyone, delighted at the turnout. She introduced me and said that I was going to talk about this other way of being Jewish that none of us even knew existed. She ended with an uptick in her voice as though I was about to take them on a magic carpet ride to an unknown kingdom full of flying horses, lounging sultans, and esoteric practices.

No such luck. I began by identifying myself as a newbie at Desert Manor, but an oldie as a Jew, which got a few appreciative chuckles. Then, I added a category they hadn't expected. I said I was a feminist Jew. With a growing chorus of whispers of,

"What does that mean?"

"What does one thing have to do with the other?"

I began by describing a conference held forty years ago as Jewish feminists began to challenge traditional Judaism. The question that framed the gathering was, "Why is this Conference different from all other Conferences?" The answer? "Because it was organized by heterosexual and lesbian feminists."

I let the confusion settle before continuing with the less bewildering story of how the orange became a part of Passover.

A woman belongs on the bima like an orange belongs on the seder plate, a rabbi scoffed after a presentation by a feminist scholar. Within a year, seder plates all over the country had oranges added to the lamb shank, horseradish, bitter herbs, and other symbols of the Passover holiday. The creaky portals of traditional Judaism were swinging open, and women were writing music, biblical interpretation, and new forms of liturgy. Chavurot were formed for groups to gather and pray, celebrate holidays and life cycle events without formal leadership. Women were being ordained, and scholars were writing books that challenged and upended conventional wisdom, exploring how gender was a necessary lens through which to understand Jewish history.

After that brief formal introduction of the feminist presence in Renewal Judaism, I took a breath and told them my origin story. It began in a conventional Reform synagogue, authoritatively led by a rabbi and cantor who stood above and before us on a bima, an image that was familiar to everyone there. The learned people, always men, were on the bima. They taught. We received.

"When I was thirteen, my parents, brother, and I were in synagogue for Yom Kippur, each of us wearing an outfit specially bought for the High Holidays. We, along with the other congregants, were participating in an unspoken and unacknowledged fashion competition; my mother wore her mink stole, my father his camel-hair coat, and I was wearing nylons, which felt both gloriously mature and extremely itchy.

The service began with the Kol Nidre, the elegiac prayer sung to usher in the day of atonement, reflection, and recommitment. The congregation rose, and I stood in my new patent leather Capezios as the cantor's voice deepened with each of the three repetitions of the prayer. At its completion, rather than return to his velvet high-backed chair, he haltingly walked off the bima. The rabbi stepped up to the microphone to continue the service, but after a few minutes, several of the temple elders hurriedly made their way down the center aisle, approached the rabbi, and whispered something in his ear. The entire congregation was alert that something was wrong and anxious whispering began to fill the congregation. Then, there was silence as the rabbi held up his hands,

"Our beloved Cantor Roshbach has died," he said. "God allowed him to offer the Kol Nidre as his last act of devotion."

It was in that moment, that I understood that God watched how we conducted ourselves. God decided when it was time to die. This was worse than being watched by my mother. At least she couldn't always see me, but if God could, there was no escape. I was sad that Cantor Roshbach had died, but for me, in that moment, if I was to have any privacy in my life, God had to go as well. So, I decided not to believe in him anymore.

Thirty years later, when my partner and I, meeting with a young gay rabbi to plan her funeral after a terminal breast cancer diagnosis (*there*, I thought, *I'm thoroughly out*), that I reached for the scaffolding that Judaism offers to the mourner.

I paused, letting my words reverberate for a minute during which no one moved, before switching gears and continuing,

"There's more to say about my relationship to Judaism at this point in my life, but what's central to Renewal and to me, is the *kavanah* (spiritual intention) with which I study and practice and pray and live. Being a Jew is something I am. Not just on Friday nights or Saturday mornings. Not just the holidays, although I love them. But my trying, although not always succeeding, to keep my heart and mind open, and maintaining a sense of wonder about the world we have been given to inhabit."

That was much more than I had intended to say. Way more. But what finally got and held their attention was when I referenced the new music that was being written and used Debbie Friedman as an example, whose videos were a part of their weekly services.

"We're already doing it," Shirley whispered delightedly, her whisper loud enough for the entire gathering to hear.

"We are partly Renewal!"

When I finished, I asked for questions or comments. Rosalyn wanted to hear more about the chavurah process and how we could study together if there wasn't a rabbi to let us know if we were right or not. Trying to avoid a long disquisition about there being no right or wrong, which I suspected was probably going to land somewhere in the blasphemous vicinity, I deflected her concern by making the old joke about two Jews, three opinions. It worked.

As everyone left the Cinema Room, I hoped the lack of reaction to my talk was because residents were hesitant to ask questions in a group setting. I had come out. I had temporarily turned my back on God. Maybe, I thought, someone would approach me in a less public situation—maybe one afternoon in the café or on the elevator. No one did.

Several days later, Malka asked if I would facilitate the Jews Schmooze every other Wednesday while she continued leading Shabbat services.

"You can teach them more about Renewal if you want to. Just for a while," she added. "Till I get back to myself."

Benny had already scheduled a screening of *Rhapsody in Blue* for the following Wednesday, primarily because Gershwin was a Jew. Then there would be me. I'd follow George. If I wanted to become a part of things, to find a way to belong, at least a little bit, I would have to cut back on the nos. I'd already racked up a no on watching movies every other Wednesday afternoon, another about having dinner in the dining room, and a third about playing bingo. I said yes.

Two weeks later, I arranged the chairs in a circle for a dozen folks, but nearly thirty arrived. It took a while to create a large enough circle, untangle the walkers, and make space for the scooters. After everyone settled down, I suggested that we silence our phones. I was, after all, the master of ceremonies, just as I had been when instructing Evan's stuffed animals to do the same. While the animals were certain to remain quiet, I discovered that many residents didn't know how to use their phones except to answer an incoming call. Turning it off and on wasn't in their repertoire. Dismay and whispering surfaced, and I hurried past the moment. Then, there was a general inability to modulate volume. There were efforts intended to be respectful, to whisper to the resident beside them, but given everyone's level of hearing, the whisper tended to be closer to full-volume speech. This resulted in a counterpoint of hissed "shhh." The soundtrack of Jewish gatherings.

I said something about how good it felt to have something to say and knowing you had everyone's attention. That's what we'll try to give one another. That feeling of full attention. I wound down my instruction, feeling too close to Malka's fifth-grade teacher voice to be comfortable. Fortunately, she wasn't there. Nor was Benny. She was either relieved that things were continuing without her, or she didn't want to see that things were continuing without her. I was relieved she wasn't there to hear my schoolmarm-ish gaffe.

I began the gathering by asking them to talk about how the way Judaism had shaped their lives. Dolly spoke first, describing her Orthodox father, who had supervised every aspect of family life.

"My mother never even said boo when he was around. She just went along with everything, no matter what it was. My whole childhood was nothing but rules. And if I knew what was good for me, I'd better follow them, because my mother never even made a peep. She didn't stick up for me or herself."

I had already heard that Dolly had married a quiet guy who let her "rule the roost." Now that she was a widow, she continued to rule her own roost and spent most of her days watching and re-watching authoritative male movie stars from the movies of the 1940s.

Shana told us about how her eager preparations for her eldest son's bar mitzvah ended when the rabbi explained that she couldn't come up on the bima.

"That's for the men," he said.

At the bar mitzvah of her second son, the rabbi said he would permit her to come up two steps toward the bima. She defied his command. Although she would never be permitted an *aliyah* (the blessing over the Torah reading), she stood beside her son before their gathered friends and family as he read his Torah portion. Shana concluded her story by saying that because of that experience, she became a Humanist Jew. There is no God in Humanism. No rabbis. No hard and fast rules. It's about being kind, fair, patient, and respectful to everyone.

"No more God baloney for me," she said firmly.

Neither Naomi nor Rosalyn followed my instructions, but first, one and then the other talked about their proud accomplishments as active members in the sisterhoods of their Chicago and Los Angeles Conservative synagogues. They talked of having been in charge of coordinating fundraisers, creating social and holiday events, running summer camp programs, and making sure that everything functioned smoothly.

Naomi concluded by saying,

"The sisterhood was a godsend, especially when the children were in school all day and there wasn't much else to do."

My sisterhood had been a godsend too. We had fundraisers, wrote books, made music, demonstrated, studied, organized, and dreamed together. Everything was accomplished by volunteers like Rosalyn and Naomi because we believed in the necessity and power of feminist values. In their case, they valued living the life of an *eishet chayil*, a woman of valor. I identified as a *vilde chaya*, a wild woman, working to upend and remake everything they held dear.

Sixteen
What Would Mrs. Maccabee Say?

As Chanukah approached, I was asked to offer a "little something" each evening before the candles were lit. A giant electric menorah took center stage at the head of a long table in the activities room. Everyone was there—everyone who was mobile. Chanukah brought out the non- and anti-religious as well as the non-schmoozers. The room was packed, and all heads turned as I entered. I was a resident Jew for whom heads would turn.

Taking my seat between Dolly and Rivka, I was immediately urged to move to the head of the table. I was considered to be a leader, someone who would create ritual moments. There had even been a Friday morning when Malka had an urgent doctor's appointment, and I stepped forward to lead the Shabbat service.

I moved to the front and cleared my throat, signaling the end of whispering and visiting. Before I could begin, Shirley offered a lengthy explanation about which direction the bulbs were supposed to be turned on.

"To the left," she said firmly.

"But why that way?" Rivka challenged.

This led to spirited dissension. The direction in which the bulbs were lit was clearly of significance and everyone had to have their point of view on the record. Once agreement had been reached, I introduced the idea of how the *shamash* (helper) served as the secretary or assisted the cantor or the hazan who led the service. It's the shamash on the menorah that brings the light without which there would be no memory or blessing. Nothing can go forward without it. That's a pretty good description of a Jewish woman, I said and paused to see where this thought might lead.

There was an enthusiastic eruption of agreement and stories about how they had been *shamashes* in their lives. They were the ones who suggested, guided, and encouraged. Everyone had been a *shamash*, and everyone had a story. I began the blessing for the lighting of the menorah, and everyone joined in. The first night was a rousing success.

On the second night, I asked a question to generate conversation.

"Why was there no Mrs. Maccabee in the story?" I asked. "How do you think she was feeling when her husband and sons went off to battle?"

The answers varied from she was proud because they were heroes, to she was angry because they were shmendricks who didn't have enough sense to hide and keep themselves safe so they could care for their families. Everyone was involved, and everyone had a strongly held point of view.

Remembering my exhilaration the first time I was called up for an *aliyah* (reciting the blessings that precede and conclude the reading of the Torah), on the third night, I encouraged anyone who wanted to offer both their own or the traditional blessing to come up to the front. People were delighted to have their moment, and I was happy to include them in this service, one with an electric candle holder in an activities room in a retirement community, yet one that held them up as special, worthy of the honor of adding their words, their blessings to this moment of illumination.

Naomi never missed a service, a Yiddish club, or any special Jewish event. Her husband had recently died, and she partnered up with Mel, which meant that they had dinner together at Benny and Malka's table, and she sat beside him when there was entertainment. She was unfailingly cheerful, even as her confusion grew, and her memory shrank. But on the fourth night, she remembered the blessing word for word. Evie and Edie or Edie and Evie always sat together at every gathering, and both said the blessing on the fifth, Malka and Benny on the sixth, Shirley on the seventh, and we all recited the blessing together with a flourish on the eighth.

A few weeks later, on January 15, 2022, a synagogue in Colleyville, Texas, was held hostage; the congregants saved only by the quick thinking and safety training of the rabbi. The national attention this attack received evoked resigned confirmation from every Schmoozer about how dangerous it was to be a Jew. Even the shy people who didn't usually speak up had something to say. Everyone, it seemed, had a strong point of view about being a Jew in America. And in the world.

"They hate us."

"They're jealous of us."

"Jews are always made to be the problem."

"They didn't want us in Europe, and they don't want us here."

While each of them was proud to be an American and believed in fair play, fair jobs, and fair schools—they were all good Democrats after all; just under the surface was the unshakable conviction that they needed to stick with their own because the world was precarious for Jews. Always had been. Always would be. They remembered growing up being told by Christian kids that they had killed Christ, been called kikes, and were assumed to be cheats and liars. Especially about money. Jews and money—always an incendiary mix.

As I listened, I remembered my mother, when learning I was preparing to demonstrate against the war in Vietnam, cautioned me to mind my own business and stay inside. Not to be a Jew in public and draw attention to myself. She felt it was dangerous, not only because I was protesting a government policy, but because it was Jewishly dangerous as well. As diligently as she had worked to apprentice herself to middle-class ways of dressing, furnishing her home and raising her children, her fear was a visceral one, an expression of the same dread that I was hearing sixty years later. For her, and for everyone in the Cinema Room, the world was treacherous for Jews, which was why they believed we needed to be watchful and support the safe haven of Israel that assured our continuity. Without challenge. Without question.

I had traveled to Israel/Palestine multiple times over the past decades, engaged with Israeli and Palestinian activists and teachers there, attended feminist conferences, and developed a critical and concerned view of who was in power, and how that power was being wielded. My history was one of advocating, demonstrating, and writing. I had questions. And challenges. About the rise of anti-Semitism in America. About the policies of the state of Israel. But in this precarious moment, I kept them to myself.

Seventeen
Too Jewish

Sunday morning services were listed on the activities sheet as non-denominational. Having already joined the Jewish prayer gatherings, I was curious about what services with the rest of the community were like, so I decided to make a joyful noise with this new crowd.

The cross in the center of the chapel was crooked. One of the stained-glass panels that hung in the windows directly facing the entrance of the facility, intended to spiritually cover the view, had lost a hinge. The piano was out of tune. The prayer books were in a closet that only two staff members had access to, and they hadn't yet arrived for work. Nonetheless, dozens of residents enthusiastically arrived with walkers, scooters, canes, and even a few like me, upright and unencumbered.

As I sat down beside Alice, a woman with whom I had broken bread (the bread in question being English muffins in the cafe), several congregants turned to look at me with curiosity, confused that a woman they thought was Jewish was there. Maybe I wasn't. But maybe I was, so why then did I attend services? So many questions. So few answers. I smiled warmly at everyone and remained quiet, understanding that "visiting," which is what

Jews do in synagogue before services begin, was not the appropriate behavior here.

The service leader bustled in, clothed in compression stockings, oxfords, a dark skirt, and a polyester blouse, welcoming us as she walked directly to the piano. She began to play "The Old Rugged Cross," and the chapel filled with quavery voices raised in thanksgiving as we made our way through several other songs, none of which I knew, all of which centered on the theme of crosses.

She told us how delighted she was to see us all gathered to praise Him. She talked about her experience of being saved when she was five, her parents' lives as ministers, and her calling to a teaching ministry. While it was clearly an oft-told tale, and undoubtedly, for many, not the first time they had heard it, her delight in how splendidly her life of service had developed was contagious.

It became apparent that I had unwittingly chosen a dramatic day to join this congregation. Jesus was being crucified. In detail. At great length. I found myself wondering how his suffering was comforting—all the flaying and smiting, the rent garments, and the blood. So much blood.

It's for our sins. I know that's the right answer for believers, but for a woman who lost track of what happened between the Old Testament and the New One, I never got clear on His transition from radical rabbi to the son of God. There are books to answer my questions, but the question itself was never sufficiently urgent to search them out.

I settled my mind down and instructed it to stop noticing, observing, and assessing, so that I could find my way into the experience that was being provided for people for whom this was ritual, history, comfort, and balm.

Keep still, I hissed silently to myself. *This is not a class in theology. Just join in.*

There was none of the usual instructions to "rise and sing" or "rise and read responsively." Maybe because this is not a population of easy risers. Or maybe this is not a service that requires rising. Maybe spirits are rising, and I just can't tell.

The service leader spoke about how the body of Christ, which was in the process of being abused, was his holy temple, or at least I think that's what she was saying. We Jews give thanks for our bodies every morning, but it's only recently that we have actual bodies in our services. There are a lot of minds. Jews love to think argue and discuss. About everything. But only in recent decades have bodies have been incorporated into prayer life. In the synagogue I attended before moving here, there was dancing, spinning, twirling—only at the relevant parts of the service of course, but still.

My mind drifted down that pathway for a while until I realized I had missed most of the homily, which appeared to be a religious parallel to the sermon service leaders offer on the week's Torah portion. Since Christ had just been crucified for the sins of the people, the homily was embedded in the forms of gratitude our lives should, therefore, express.

Kindness, love, appreciation for what we have, and sharing our bounty with others—it all seems to end up in pretty much the same place, I thought—my mind taking center stage yet again. With all the traditions—Christian, Buddhist, Baptist, Muslim, Hindu, and Sikh—reaching for our best selves is always the goal.

Ok, my mind continued. *But how does getting a hold of one's best self begin to translate into the daily lives of these old parishioners? What are the teachings about managing their lives now? Their failing bodies. Their loneliness.*

I snapped back to attention as cups were being passed out for the taking of communion. Decades before, I had attended midnight mass services in a large urban church and witnessed hundreds of people lined up to take communion with great ceremonial pomp and circumstance. This second communion experience was an infinitely humbler affair with little plastic cups of wine accompanied by a plate of torn bread. No pomp. Not a single circumstance. Yet, watching the congregants prayerfully ingest the blood and the body of Jesus was imbued with the same solemnity as it had been for the worshippers in New York City.

I glanced over at Alice, who remained unmoving, her palms on her lap. Her stillness communicated a deep sense of privacy that inhibited me from looking directly at her. After communion, the collection plate was passed, which I suspect was intended to augment whatever small sum this woman was being paid to provide services. Most days, I no longer carry anything except my phone in case I fall, not because I'm going to receive important calls I cannot miss. I don't have any more of those. But I had neither my phone nor my wallet because I had no money to offer and thought of leaning over and asking Alice to put in a couple of bucks for me, and I'd return it later in the day but didn't because it just felt too...Jewish.

Eighteen
First Visit Back

After the deluge of festivities that included Chanukah, Christmas, and New Year's Eve, which ended at 10:00 pm to correspond with New York midnight and allowed residents to adhere to their usual bedtime, I was chafing for a break from institutional celebrations. I missed my friends, and while we tried to sustain our intimacy with Zoom, much as we all had during COVID, it simply wasn't the same as being together. I'd begin my first year at Desert Manor with a return to the Bay Area.

I began preparing for my return trip, and since I always overpack when I'm worried, my unease about how things might go became replaced by how many sweaters I'd need and what if it rains. Returning to the world I had so precipitously exited left me so anxious and overprepared that I had to check my bag because it wouldn't fit in the overhead. I had clothing for every weather eventuality and the remote possibility that all the drugstores would abruptly close. Toothpicks. Dental floss. Alka Seltzer. Hand cream. Where did I think I was going? I was protecting myself from a never-gonna-happen drugstore emergency to avoid the real worry I had about how I'd feel when I got there.

What would it be like to see the friends I had left just three months ago? I wanted our connection to be as immediate as it had always been, even though I knew that wasn't realistic. Just as I was making a daily life without them, they were doing the same without me. Would there be a series of halting moments between us, an awkward need to reestablish ourselves across the separation I had created? When they asked what Phoenix was like, it would be easy to describe the irrational politics, the desert flora and fauna, the pleasures of being near my daughters, and the details of adjustments. But they'd want to know more about what it was like to be me in this unfamiliar life, just as I would have had the situation been reversed.

I didn't know how to describe my life with the honesty they would want and deserve without revealing my sense of shame about what I'd done. Maybe they were as eager as I was not to open the can of worms that was my leave-taking. Feelings might spill out, and once expressed, wouldn't change anything but instead deepen my sense of regret. I'd have to wait and see, the most vulnerable way to go into an emotionally complicated situation.

As the plane made its way to the Bay Area, I felt a rising sense of possibility that maybe, just maybe, I could have both a continuation of my life there, along with the building of a new one in Phoenix. Perhaps I could figure out a way to juggle everything.

Pulling my overpacked suitcase to the exit of the familiar airport, I gave myself a little talk, which is what I do when I'm scared. *You'll be fine. However this turns out, you'll have clarity and be able to stop wondering if you made the right choice and adjust to what is.* That was the extent of the talk, but it was enough to get me into the Lyft and heading to Nan's house, where I was to stay with her and Jonathan.

Welcomed with their usual warmth and enthusiasm, we sat down to one of Nan's multi-course, elaborate, and glorious dinners. Over curried pumpkin soup, poached salmon, rice pilaf, and steamed asparagus, I told them about Shana and Shirley, Rivka and Mel, giving them a glimpse into that part of my life. But I kept my loneliness tucked away, even with Nan, one of my closest friends, a woman who has known me for thirty-five years. The reality was that I ate dinner by myself every night, that except for Marion, there wasn't anyone I could talk politics with, that I didn't find Phoenix appealing, even though I took myself to the independent bookstore, museums, and art galleries hoping to create the kind of urban life I was used to, remained stuck in my throat. I just wasn't ready or able to hear myself say any of that out loud.

Instead, I asked about their lives and caught up with what they were doing. When it was finally bedtime, I relievedly excused myself and climbed the stairs to my room.

The following morning, I drove my rental car to my old neighborhood, uneasy about seeing my apartment house again. Parking the car, I stood across the street, looking up at the once-familiar building. Since my departure, it had been repainted from a warm golden color to a flat white, which left it looking like second-rate brutalist architecture. My top-floor window was covered with hanging plants, which obscured the once glorious view from within the enclosed patio. Nothing looked as it had--

which felt unexpectedly freeing. Everything hadn't remained the same and gone on without me. Both it and I had changed.

I moved from the sidewalk to the path along the water to the pier, a walk I had taken for decades. There were so many memories still alive here. The companionable early morning strolls I had taken with friends before we headed off to the Sconehenge Café or La Note for breakfast. My urgent tempo as I walked at dawn during the pandemic. The strenuous exercise to get my body ready for surgery, and the halting steps while pushing a rollator afterward. The benches where I had sat and read and daydreamed. All that rich history swirled around me as I walked the familiar landscape.

I arranged to meet a friend for lunch or dinner each day I was there, and as I drove to meet them, every highway exit became a portal bringing rushes of memories. I took the Grand Avenue exit to see Donna and walk around Lake Merritt. Park Boulevard, to have lunch with Elana at Buccinos, the only café with an outdoor table so she could bring her little dog, Alice B. Toklas. College Avenue to see Nancy and Frankie, Diesel Books, the movie theater, and the Chinese restaurant. The 35th St. exit for Rochelle and Eva. Edwards Avenue for Lorraine. The unspooling highway, a map of my history.

As I sat across the table from my dear ones catching up with our lives, I described the residents and their interactions with me, the Jewish life that was available there, but said little about how I felt about living at Desert Manor. Instead, I finessed their questions by saying I was finding my way, it was a difficult adjustment, and other distancing euphemisms that didn't fool anybody. But my friends were kind and didn't push past where I was willing to go. They listened to my stories, laughed at the funny parts, sighed at the realities of institutional dining room culture and the centrality of bingo, and continued to love me. As they always had.

I was reassured by their response. I wasn't ready for much more honesty. Neither my own nor theirs. I still felt too exposed as the impulsive woman I'd been when I left my life to begin a new one. The fear that fueled my move was replaced with a longing for what I'd left. A life where I had been held as I mourned the death of my beloved at fifty and supported when I stopped drinking at sixty. When first my brother, and then when my mother died. When I fell off a raised platform at a demonstration, landing with a bone-breaking splat on the concrete sidewalk. In the haze of my pain, I sensed that there was a woman in the ambulance with me, later, another sleeping on my sofa, and yet a third taking care of medications and sponge baths. I had political buddies, jazz buddies, travel buddies, and talking everything-over buddies. My life had been cushioned by their care and their love.

Returning to Phoenix, Alison met me with a cooler filled with my dinner and a bouquet of tulips. I nearly wept but didn't let myself because she wouldn't have understood my confusion of sorrow and gratitude.

Nineteen
Changing the World is Not a Solo Activity

Marion led a meeting about politics, which usually had four or five people in attendance. She talked in granular detail about the upcoming races and the issues that were at stake to a group of residents who already felt their political obligations were fulfilled when they voted as their family always had. Straight Democratic. No further information was necessary. It would be an uphill climb to create some energy around her meeting, but I wanted to try.

At one of our lunches, I suggested some ways she might gin up more enthusiasm for what seemed to be her extremely valuable presentations. Maybe we could design fliers letting folks know about the monthly gathering beyond what was listed in the elevators. We could organize discussion groups and create concrete tasks like writing postcards or making calls. Work old people could do while sitting down. When I paused and looked across the table, she said, "I can't do activist stuff like my dad did. It's just not me." She took a breath and continued. "I just want to tell them what I have learned about the politics here. What they do about it is up to them."

"Of course," I quickly replied. "Just a thought," I concluded with a casualness that I hoped eased her discomfort.

She switched gears by asking me about my activism before I moved into Desert Manor. I was delighted for the opportunity to tell her about Women in Black, Jewish Voice for Peace, and the range of political and lesbian activist organizations that shaped my life. She marveled at my history, read copies of the one-pagers we handed out to passers-by at our demonstrations, and sighed, "My father would have loved to have been a part of something like that."

While my organizing days appeared to have ground to a halt, an unexpected conversation over a lunch of tuna fish in the café moved me briefly back into the fray.

I was sitting with Rivka, a woman who was widely known as someone stubbornly dedicated to sticking up for herself which I knew had been a hard-won freedom for women of our generation. We were joined by Irene, who sat at Shirley's table where Rivka wasn't welcome, carrying an egg salad sandwich so she could eat her own food, the only food she trusted. The two women, both with brightly hennaed hair, Rivka's in red and Irene's one shade darker (they both went to the beautician who worked on site), picked up their exchange where they had left off days before.

Rivka began this round with a challenge.

"You need to change your mind about this. There are no two ways around it. It's only because of HIPPA. When somebody dies or goes to the hospital, we never hear a word about it. It's like people disappear. They're not allowed to tell us anything. Only the family is told."

"It's called privacy," Irene responded. "Maybe some people care about privacy more than others," she warned with her tone.

"What's the privacy for when you live with people every single day? Why would you want to keep that kind of thing from them?" Rivka countered."

'We're not the family," Irene maintained, keeping the conversational ball in the air.

"But we're their everyday people. The ones who care about them, who bring them magazines and go to see them when they're too tired to come downstairs. A lot of them have families who don't even come. They shouldn't have the final say," Rivka insisted.

I leaned back in my chair and watched them bat the HIPPA dilemma around as they finished their sandwiches, concluding with a smiling,

"See you at dinner."

I suspected that this was one small bit of organizing I could manage. That and the inability to recycle anywhere in the complex were the two issues at the top of my abbreviated political agenda.

Not clear about the lines of authority and responsibility, I began close to the top—with Aaron. I didn't try to catch him as he was making his way across the lobby or the common room. I asked for an appointment designed to signal the seriousness of the conversation I intended to have.

Two days later, I entered his small, crowded office, and as I sat down on the leather chair facing his desk, I saw a picture of him with another man and a boy. It was clearly a family photo. Before my mind could take me into the muddy waters of what it might be like for him to have Mel as his dad, I decided to identify myself as a lesbian in a sea of straight old people. We would bond. He would be open to amending the HIPPA policy. This was going to be a success.

I did and it wasn't.

"How old is your son?" I began, to let him know I had seen the photo.

"He's in his last year of high school," he replied in a voice that did not encourage further questions.

"Ah," I said with a too-broad smile. Understanding I had to transition from family life, I tried, "And having your dad here must be a comfort."

"It is."

"How long have you been managing Desert Manor?"

"About two years. Just after COVID."

At the end of each answer, his face resettled into stillness. More inert than alert.

My charm, warmth, and curiosity were not going to move the conversation forward. He was a rulebound, humorless man, a bureaucrat.

I shifted gears and said that recycling simply required a specifically labeled bin in each trash room. *How hard could that be,* I thought. I understood that some of the residents wouldn't use it or be confused about what went where, and the recycling bin might end up filled with garbage, but I went on, we could have clear illustrations to help them.

His response was to explain that an ongoing study was being conducted to estimate the amount and type of recyclable waste dumped throughout Arizona, the economic impact that recycling could have, and the cost-benefit of operating recycling programs depending on communities' size and finances. He would get back to me when the study was complete. Trying to hold his attention, I said, "There's one more thing. I've heard concerns from several residents that there is no system of community notification when someone becomes ill and is taken to the hospital. Or even more painfully, when someone dies. They understand the HIPPA constraints, but I wonder if there isn't some policy that might be implemented that allows them to have access to, at least, general information about people who have been their friends, sometimes for years."

"We're not legally able to release medical information without the permission of the family," his impatient response.

"Can we figure out a form that families might sign giving permission?" my voice rising with frustration.

"I'll get back to you on that as well," he concluded.

I rose, thanked him, and left his office. Nothing changed; residents continued to disappear, information only trickling back days after they were taken to the hospital or the funeral home.

While I made repeated attempts to write to the relevant government officials asking for the financial recycling cost-benefit analysis reports, there was no response. I had hit a bureaucratic dead end. No one was ever going to get back to me.

Dispiritedly, I drove my recycling to my daughter's residential barrel twenty minutes away. Organizing needs people. It's not a solo activity. Shifting the ways things are requires pressure, leverage, and presence. I needed a gang of angry, determined old women. That might have worked. But just me by myself? I didn't have a chance.

Twenty
Facing Forward

On the first Tuesday of the month, the Avon lady came to Desert Manor to set up her wares on the edge of what also served as the dance floor. I watched her unpack and artfully arrange moisturizers, emollients, creams, sprays, balms, and polish. Within minutes, there was a crowd in front of the display as women, their eyes no longer what they used to be, leaned in to read the small print on the boxes. Later that afternoon, I saw a woman who always wore bright red lipstick, so assumed other facially decorative items accompanied her painted mouth and asked if she had bought makeup that afternoon.

"Oh, no, she replied, I don't drive anymore," The loss of her license was the slippery slope from no longer driving, to no longer getting dressed up, to no longer wearing makeup.

But I drove, and while my face had aged more gradually than most of my friends, and I found ways to mention how old I was so I could delight in people's either real or more recently perhaps, feigned astonishment at the high number, my face continued to rearrange itself into serious oldness.

As a young woman, I had emphasized and decorated my eyes. I lined and mascaraed them, remembering never to rub them when they itched because the carefully crafted effect shifted from sparkling to blurry and smeary. Which is not a good look at any age.

I eventually gave up eye makeup because I kept forgetting about the rubbing thing and remembering to buy the liner and wand that were the tools of my abbreviated trade. So, for the past thirty years, nothing has been added to my face to alter, augment, or improve it.

But during the COVID years, I began to see my father's face superimposed onto mine in my computer's Zoom square. And I didn't like it. I mean, I liked my dad fine, but an old male face with random brown spots isn't ever what I wanted at the top of my neck.

Alison, who still has most of her original face, thought it would be a splendid idea to arrange a session with a professional makeup artist; a woman would teach me how to create a painted replica of my face before it fell into disarray.

The process began with me in a salon chair facing a mirror with my bare face returning my disappointed gaze. My illustrator was holding a palette easel next to a table with a large builder's toolbox that slid open to reveal shelves of tiny jars, tubes, brushes, wands, pencils, powder, and creams in dozens of shades for every skin color. I was to be the canvas.

She assessed me with a surgically precise gaze, reached into her supplies, and daubed something on my forehead, nose, cheeks, and chin and began using a feathery brush to blend it in. Which felt like little raindrops on my face. I relaxed and imagined myself as Sandra Bullock being made up for her triumphant entrance in *Miss Congeniality*.

"This is just to moisturize your skin," she said. "And now we begin," echoing Philip Roth's famous last sentence in his then scandalous book about Portnoy, which snapped me out of movie star relaxation and into seeing myself as Roth would have seen me, scorched in what I imagined to be his scorn. An old woman having her face painted in a small studio on a busy street in a mid-sized American town. Think of what he could do with that!

But having had decades of practice casting out male thinking and assessment, I managed to do it once again. I reanimated my Sandra Bullock fantasy, Philip Roth fading into the ether, evaporating in his own misogyny.

Nearly an hour later, after her eventual final pat, smooth, and spray, my face still had every one of its deep lines, but there were no more brown spots and truly imposing crème brûlée eyes.

Alison returned me to Desert Manor after lovingly giving me a gift bag she had purchased that contained all the products that had been used to redesign my face. As I walked through the lobby, I received several puzzled glances, which got Shirley's attention, and she turned around from her bingo bar stool and hollered across the entire room,

"Are you OK?"

Did I look like I had been in a fight and ended up with two black eyes? The crème brûlée may have darkened. I certainly didn't look like I had when I'd left. Everyone turned around and stared at my unfamiliar heavily decorated appearance. The game paused as I embarrassedly and hurriedly made my way through the great room. Averting my face as best I could, I assured all of them with a clipped,

"I'm fine."

But I wasn't fine. I wanted to look like myself again, even if that meant looking like my father with brown spots. I wanted to take all that stuff off my face but didn't own any makeup remover. Why would I? My initial application of Pond's cold cream just smushed everything into a slippery, thick, multicolored coating. Rubbing with tissues merely spread it around. I resorted to the one thing I have used all my adult life. I scrubbed my face with soap. But not just any soap. French milled soap. I don't know what milling does to a bar of soap except make it more expensive, but it's from the south of France and brings back memories of my summers there. Which, of course, has nothing to do with my face.

I lathered up and began scouring, rubbing, splashing, getting water all over my shirt and the counter, but relieved as I began to see more and more of my wrinkled, brown-spotted skin. As I finished, I smiled at my happily breathing face, gathered all my new wands and tubes, and put them into a beautiful vase, which would be their permanent resting place.

Twenty-One
Geriatric Dancing

Each day's schedule was displayed throughout all the public spaces. A woman who sat on the residents' council was responsible for sliding the calendar into the plastic slot on the wall of all the elevators at the end of each day. She was proud of her responsibility and the accompanying status of being privy to what was coming before everyone else. Whenever she was approached with eager questions about when an event was to be scheduled, she always shut down the questioning resident by saying,

"I'll post it on the elevators the night before like I always do."

What remained of individual autonomy in institutional life were decisions about which activities to attend. That's what was left of our independence. Many residents clung to it, determined to create an environment as close to the one they had left behind as possible. I wondered if any of them felt relief at having their days preplanned. These were old people who had shaped their personal lives, their work lives, their parenting lives, their economic lives, and were probably tired of shaping, and willing to be shaped. At least most of the time. As did I just a few months ago.

Each morning, I reviewed the offerings on the elevator walls, although there was little that interested me. One exception was the entertainment, usually scheduled at 3:00 to account for, I suspected, both lunch and a nap. There were magicians, jugglers, groups of senior singers, baton twirlers, tap dancers, and piano players, both jazz, cabaret, and classical, all trained and very good. These local artists were grateful to have a venue for their performances, and Desert Manor needed to entertain its residents. It was a perfect fit.

The staff's primary function on days without scheduled entertainment was to get everyone up and moving, at least as much moving as was individually possible. They set up their technology in front of the piano; for some, just a microphone and speaker system, and for others, a screen where lyrics were displayed—what was once called "follow the bouncing ball." The open space became a dance floor, large enough to accommodate wheelchairs and enthusiastic staff inviting the residents to join them. These entertainments were well attended, even resulting in a bit of dress-up.

The first time I joined the audience, I sat down beside a woman who was boisterously singing with the mostly out-of-tune crowd while the mic was being passed around so everyone could have their opportunity for a solo. She accepted her moment in the spotlight with a shy pleasure, singing the words on the TV screen and joining Neil Diamond in singing "Sweet Caroline." A woman sitting across from me in the shapeless circle wobbled to her feet, holding tightly to her walker as she moved her hips and bent her knees, her face embellished with a delighted smile.

"Let Me Call You Sweetheart" was up next, and the mic was passed to a woman who remained seated on her scooter belting out the lyrics, while a rangy woman beside her danced, punctuated by vivacious arm raises and an intermittent foot lift meant to suggest a kick. A small kick, but still. While I would have chosen more Aretha and less Barry Manilow, the pleasures of singing and adaptive dancing allowed everyone to find their way to their unique forms of rocking and rolling, even if the rock was more of a sway and the roll an imperceptible shift.

Not all the residents moved slowly and deliberately. There were a half dozen scooter drivers whose speed evoked their younger days behind the wheel. While some skirted chair legs and groups of people with skillful economy, there were those who careened, driving with one hand on the wheel, calling out hellos as they whizzed past not watching what passed here for the road. I imagined them in their Chevys, radio on, cigarette in their hand resting on the open window frame, singing along with the radio and hurrying to the next exhilarating moment of their still emerging lives. Now, they danced with their vehicles.

One afternoon, an aide made her way over to where I was seated and invited me to join the party. Back in the day, when people held one another to dance, I rhumba-ed and foxtrotted like a pro. But eventually dancing became more of a solo activity, although presumably, you were paired with another who was somewhere nearby. I twisted, did the Monkey, the Watutsi, even the Mashed Potato, although I no longer remember what that one was. I loved to dance, and I loved being good at it. I unabashedly flung myself onto every dance floor that presented itself, accessing my inner James Brown.

My knees are titanium now, my left shoulder no longer rotates, and whatever I do is a faint approximation of how I once boogied. So, I hesitated when the aide reached out to bring me into the gyrating geriatric throng. Most of my recent getting down has been happily accomplished sitting in my chair and waving my shoulders and arms around while my feet and legs remain at rest. That doesn't feel like so much of a limitation; my shoulders go up and down, my fingers click, and my hips are fabulous. But then my hips have always been fabulous. It's the legs they're attached to that limit what they might be otherwise capable of doing. I've accepted that what I do is still called dancing. It's old dancing. And I've learned to be good with that. But it's something I do in private, so, I demurred. But even as I said no, I was disappointed in myself.

As soon as I returned upstairs, I took off my sneakers (no one can dance in sneakers), put on the Four Tops, and attempted to re-create the years I danced to Motown. I began to move, and I remembered myself at once. Such pleasure in my body. Such cool moves. Such tremendous hipness. But my oomph evaporated somewhere around the end of thirty-two bars. I sat down to catch my breath. Just for a minute, after which I rose to re-enter the groove. Which had the same outcome. Thirty-two bars appeared to be the maximum longevity of my hip coolness.

There was once a time when I danced till well past midnight. Then, as my youth and, later, my middle age evaporated, my range dropped to the length of an album. Now it appeared I couldn't even make it all the way through a song. Well, I could if I sat down, swayed back and forth in rhythm, snapping my fingers as if something was going on in the movement department. If that's the case, so be it. I'll sit and sway and snap my fingers, my groove undaunted. And next time I'll join the gyrating geriatric throng.

Twenty-Two
Unintended Side Effects

Aaron had only been working at Desert Manor for a few years. During his short tenure, he had begun to put all the new Jewish residents in apartments near one another. I don't think he purposefully intended to create a Jewish corridor, one that Shana turned into a vibrant Quarter, but inadvertently, he did. That, however, left the Jews who had moved into Desert Manor before his arrival scattered all over the first and second floors.

Led by Rivka, they mounted a backlash. Their corridors were empty, and they and their equally upset non-Jewish neighbors became angrily vocal at the monthly residents' meetings about the unfairness of having empty walls. They wanted what we had: a beautiful corridor studded with Shana's depictions of Jewish life. Well, at least the Jews did. The non-Jewish residents wanted decorations.

Shana and I strategized how to approach Aaron with a request to find an unused space to set up her art supplies and easel so she could produce colorful abstract images for the independent living hallways. He went for it, wanting to head off the growing chorus of complaints. After more than fifteen years of retirement, Shana happily spent her days painting and enjoying her public role as Desert Manor's resident artist.

She'd either had many marriages, or one marriage and several love affairs—I'm not sure, but there were several male names at the center of her domestic stories. There were also four sons from what appeared to have been a rotten husband who didn't leave her money when he died. And he had a fortune. Something like that.

Shana identified with me as an accomplished woman who, like her, had traveled and experienced a wider world than the primarily domestic one of the other residents. She was also the best dresser at Desert Manor, and even with her advanced scoliosis, the quality of her outfits signaled her sophistication. Once, when I complimented her on the smooth-as-a-babies-behind skin on her ninety-one-year-old face, she explained that her mother taught her,

"If you ever get to have an expensive leather sofa, you'll need to take care of it. In the meanwhile, your face is that sofa."

And it was a splendid sofa.

She told me about her early years, small-town married life, and finally, her decades as an artist. Her lovers. The applause and awards. Those were rich and full years for her, and I was pleased to be the recipient of her memories.

One afternoon, as she was regaling me with tales of her trip to Paris, where she rented a studio for the summer and met all kinds of interesting people, she said, "There were what you call people of color and lesbians and heiresses. Everybody!" she concluded triumphantly.

"Well, you know another lesbian," I responded, "Me." Then, I waited for her to absorb this unexpected piece of information.

After a long moment, she beamed and said, "Well, good for you!"

I trusted she was indicating her open-mindedness and nodded. The nearly fifty years I had been a lesbian activist appeared to be, like Shana's Parisian adventures, something firmly in the past. My primary identity here was old. Everything had collapsed into that.

Sitting in her living room, surrounded by her paintings of ample sturdy women at kitchen tables, leaning over stoves, drinking tea, deep in conversation, I wondered if any of them had been lesbians. Of course, they would have been lesbians in a 1900s kind of way. Full of unidentifiable longings. The desire to gently place their palm against a soft cheek. Glances that went on just a bit too long. Yearnings to press their body against one like their own. The opportunities for sexual contact between the immigrant women in Shana's paintings were, in the crowded living environments of the shtetl and early immigrant life, too limited— privacy not available to the poor.

Lesbians have been a part of every generation, century, and community, just invisible to others, and often to ourselves. Was I to become invisible after fifty years? No, I most decidedly was not. I began to pay close attention to my pronouns, using 'she' when I talked about my partners and what I referred to as my adventures. What surprised me was that there were no questions. Either there was no curiosity about having a full-fledged lesbian in their midst, which seemed unlikely, or they were reticent to ask the inevitable question lesbians of my generation confront.

"Do you hate men?"

No one asked. The answer would have begun with no, then moved to what I hoped would be a clear and kind explanation about masculinity. But the opportunity never arose. Instead, the unintended side effect was that in referring to the death of my female partner and the book we wrote together, I became a person with whom it was OK to talk about death. Perhaps I might be someone open to conversations that were otherwise too difficult to have.

Wives talked about their dead husbands reverentially, all the pushes and pulls of decades of domestic life smoothed over into a series of pastel memories. Husbands of women who had died didn't talk at all, although they listened. We were all old, and as sad as it was to lose one's life partner, it was to be expected. But a few of the residents had lost a child, and because I had written about a death that was out of order, the women who needed to talk about their child found me.

Ada and Jerry had chosen to live at the Desert Manor, loved to tell everyone that they were second cousins just to see the looks on their faces, were in their late seventies, in good health, and she described her life as being in camp all year round. She played ping pong and pool, took dancing and art classes, sang on karaoke nights, enjoyed bingo, was in the audience for every performer, ate in the dining room at Malka and Benny's table, and was having the time of her life. Her hair was purple, and her clothing consisted of a collection of Outback animal prints. Except that she had a son she felt she could never mention. Once, when I asked her about him, she said she was careful never to bring the subject up.

"It would make people feel bad. Nobody wants to talk about kids who die."

"What was his name?" I asked.

"Not here. Can we talk in your apartment where it's more private?"

"Of course, we can," I replied, as we left the café, and made our silent way along the hall, up the elevator, and down the corridor to my apartment.

As soon as we got inside, she said, "His name was Daniel. Daniel Glassman. He was thirty-three when he took his life."

"Tell me about Daniel," I said. And she did. Her memories erupted, memories she had kept private, his life unknown and unseen by the people with whom she was sharing the last decades of her life. His passion for Mallomars as a child, his crush on a girl in junior high named Ada (isn't that a funny coincidence, she added), and his growing interest in psychology.

"Daniel always had depression, and when I think back, I just didn't know how to handle it. I didn't understand it was a disease like they do nowadays. I just kept trying to get him to feel better, to have fun, to lighten up."

Her voice dropped to a whisper. "I feel so guilty," as she began to sob.

Every few days, Ada came to my apartment, a safe space where she could remember her boy. Then, through an invisible grapevine, Rosalyn approached me and asked if we could talk. She emphasized the word talk with such determination, I understood at once and asked her to come to my apartment for a cup of tea that afternoon.

Her son Reuben had been six when he died. He was a twin, but the only one with cancer.

I was in therapy for ten years afterward," she began. "I wouldn't have been able to come through and care for my living son if I hadn't. Those sessions saved my life."

"Tell me about Reuben," I said. That was all I needed to say. My living room was an oasis where Rosalyn and Ada didn't have to worry about upsetting me, dampening the mood of people enjoying an activity, or being singled out as everyone's worst everyone's worst nightmare. A mother whose child had died.

I was never visible as a lesbian at Desert Manor, but I was the old woman they talked to about their dead children.

Twenty-Three
The Memory of Touch

"You can call me Reb Dov if you want to," he suggested playfully as we sat down at the café table. After spending more than a dozen Shabbat and Shmooze gatherings with him, this was the first time we had spoken to one another. As he settled into his chair, I said I'd be happy to call him Reb Dov and asked him what brought him to Desert Manor. He began at the end.

"My children took away my apartment, sold my car, and put me here with an allowance that's not even enough to buy presents for my grandchildren. None of my three children would give me even a bedroom upstairs in their homes."

My benign question had unwittingly hit a nerve for him, and I tried to shift the focus of his disappointment. I asked why they thought living here was a better idea, and he described a very bad "episode," which landed him in the emergency room, after which he returned to his daughter's house for ten days. Clearly, what happened was considerably more than very bad although he was unclear about the medical specifics. Then, he continued, on the eleventh day, "I was deposited here."

With that, his face tightened, and he abruptly pushed himself up from the chair, straightened his yarmulke, said he'd see me tomorrow, and walked back to the empty studio apartment into which his children had consigned him.

A week later, in a snippet of overheard conversation, I learned that Dov had never had a bar mitzvah, and wouldn't it be terrific if we could get him one—like a bar mitzvah for an 86-year-old man was gettable, like a prune Danish at the nearest deli.

When I next saw him leaving the dining room on a Sunday afternoon, I caught up with him and asked if he had a minute. His face wreathed with smiles, and he said, using the endearment with which he always addressed me, "Of course, my little communist. I always have time for you."

I raised the question about a bar mitzvah carefully, asking what denomination was the best fit for him.

"I don't have one because I don't think there is a God, but I believe there's something. There must be. Just look around," he said. "*Gan Eden*, the paradise to come, has to be here. I almost died in surgery, and I'm here to tell you there is nothing after we die. Nothing. It was all darkness. Emptiness. Nothing. So, we have to have our paradise while we're alive."

Then he ducked his head, not quite meeting my eyes. He whispered,

"What I want is not a bar mitzvah. I want a girlfriend. Maybe I should make a tee shirt that says on the front, 'I am looking for a girlfriend.' And on the back, too," he added laughingly.

My schemes about organizing a bar mitzvah evaporated and I said,

"Well, Dov, I can't be your girlfriend, but perhaps I can become your matchmaker," knowing already it was a doomed enterprise. He had no money and not much health. He was merely a lonely, tender, eager man.

Shirley told me that after her husband died, there was someone who had been interested in her, but she wasn't going to take a chance on being a nurse or a purse for some old guy. Nobody will want to be a nurse or a purse for Dov. He swims every single day—naked. I imagine it's how he gives his skin pleasure. Some of the residents whose windows overlook the pool have called management to complain—although I suspect others look forward to watching him.

Women who work in senior facilities often report that their clients inappropriately reach for a hug or a kiss when they're showering or getting dressed. The assumption is that there is something predatory about the impulse to reach for human touch. While I'm certain that is true in some cases, old bodies continue to long to be held in a kind embrace. But there are few opportunities for that, so men, and probably some women, create moments where they can satisfy their hunger for contact. I understood the impulse and sometimes sensed that when I hugged my daughters hello or goodbye, I held on for a beat or two longer than might be comfortable for them.

One morning, as I walked through the lobby, I saw Dov sitting alone on a bench just outside the sliding doors, and I joined him. He eagerly stood up to embrace me, and I let him, identifying with an isolated old man who simply wanted to press his body against another's. Feeling the full body contact of another human being is a comfort, and old people who live alone don't get to experience it. Like Dov. Like me.

Twenty-Four
Goodbye and Thank You

On an ordinary Tuesday morning, as I was preparing to make dutiful circles around the building, Alison called to tell me that Wally had begun what she described as "actively dying." Would I meet her in the lobby of his facility and come upstairs with her? Of course, I would.

Wally was ninety-nine and had been failing for months. I'd visited him often, sometimes accompanied by a daughter and at others by myself. I liked just the two of us alone better.

I'd been too young, too inexperienced, too unformed to be the wife he thought he'd married, and the ending of our marriage sixty years before had badly wounded him. But during the decades of his much more successful marriage with Rita that followed ours, and again after her death, I'd felt the need to revisit the history of our divorce, first in a carefully crafted letter and then in a series of conversations. He deserved my apology, and I wanted to offer it.

Now we were both old and all of that seemed so long ago. Wally knew my body and I knew his. We knew one another's parents, histories, and losses. And we were both coming to the end of our lives in the same city, accompanied by our daughters. A return to the original shape of our young lives. He had always said he wanted to live to be one hundred and in his recent years teasingly followed that with,

"Then you and I will get remarried to celebrate and the girls can give you away." He would throw his head back and laugh with a heartiness he could only intermittently summon. He didn't make it. We didn't remarry. But because of the mercies of his failing mind, he thought we had.

Our daughters patiently accompanied his decline. They took him for drives, punctuated by his long-awaited martini. They sang "My Way" and "In The Wee Small Hours of the Morning" with him as he told them stories about his life. They were always the same stories, but the girls received them with kindness. He had been a complicated father, and they had both, in their own ways, forgiven the ways he had disappointed them. I was grateful that he would be ushered out of his life with such care and that, eventually, I too, could look forward to the same loving attention and forgiveness. This was why I was in Phoenix, after all, watching a dress rehearsal for my own exit. His small apartment was in a place. They could try to dress it up with fancy words like residence, complex, campus, Splendido or Marvella, but it was and would always be a place—a transitory environment in which old people ended their lives.

I drove to Sunrise Village to find Alison waiting in the lobby, looking scared, resolute, and young. We went upstairs together, down the long-carpeted hallway, past the doors haphazardly decorated as they were in the Desert Manor with representations of the residents' individuality, a distinctiveness that was a remnant of their pasts. Wally's was a cartoon of a man drinking a martini. I no longer remember the punchline.

I pushed open the door into the darkened living room. Wally was in the hospital bed, his aide rising as we entered.

"I'll be right outside if you need me," she whispered.

And there he was. The man who had laughingly twirled me in a rhumba at our wedding. The man with whom I had two daughters. The man who had taken me across the threshold into adulthood.

His room was filled with the inescapable artifacts of dying. Pads with scrawled notes spilled over every surface, tangled with cat toys, pencils, remotes, and abandoned magazines. Containers of Ensure piled up by the refrigerator. Boxes of Depends by the bathroom.

The shades were drawn, and his breathing had become a rasp. I pulled a chair up to the side of his bed, sat down, and wrapped my hands around his. As I leaned over to kiss him goodbye, I remembered sitting beside my mother at her sister's gravesite as she reached for my hand whispering, "There's nobody left who knew me when I was young. I'm by myself now" With Wally's death, there would no longer be anyone who had known me when I was young. I was left to carry my history alone.

"Thank you, Wally, I said. Thank you for our years together, for our beautiful daughters, and for your presence in our lives over these decades. I will miss you."

I embraced Alison who, along with Janaea, would remain beside him until his death. As I left, she settled into the Lazy-Boy beside his bed, reached for his hand and nodded goodbye to me.

Driving back to Desert Manor, my thoughts returned to my mother, and her death twenty-five years before. Like Wally, she had been living in a place when she began to die. She'd fallen three times in as many days and was taken to the hospital, aching and dehydrated. Even there, her fierce insistence on going home, wherever she imagined home to be, fueled her energy to try and climb over the bars enclosing her. I imagined her bony splotched leg swinging over the metal barrier, her crumple on the cold linoleum. Did she call out for a nurse? Whimper for her mother?

If she did, no one heard her, and it wasn't until the nurse came in on her rounds that my mother was "found on the floor." After that, there was a monitor on the bed to protect my mother from her powerful longing to escape this last narrow confinement.

Then it was just us in a sterile room. She slept, morphine in her IV, her breath even and steady. Her arms were swollen and bruised from all the needles that had been inserted into her thin wrinkled skin, so like mine, skin that always bruised so easily. I watched the rise and the fall of her narrow chest and synchronized my breath to hers. Once my mother and I were a complete creature, I embedded deeply within her body. Now, again, our breath rose and fell in unison.

I sat quietly beside her, her eyes partially open, her gaze milky and unfocused. Her hands and feet were turning blue, her pulse was low, and her breathing increasingly labored. I rested my hand lightly on her chest as it rose and fell, murmuring words that tumbled out of my lips until they were gone, and the room was again still. I kissed her slightly parted lips, her eyes, open and unseeing, her papery cheek.

"Goodbye, Ma," I whispered. "Thank you for my life."

My daughters will witness, accompany, and grieve this flawed, tender man who had been their father, just as I had with their grandmother.

How blessed he is to be surrounded by his daughters. I'll need that blessing when it's my time. This—near my girls—is where I belong.

Twenty-Five
Crossing the Red Sea

Every holiday season, whether secular, religious, or patriotic, the lobby of the Desert Manor was decorated with relevant artifacts, images, and exuberant signage. As we approached Easter, Shirley took serious umbrage at what she saw as a slap in her Jewish face.

"How come they have bunnies and Easter egg baskets all over the tables, and there isn't a single slice of matzoh anywhere?" she complained to anyone who would listen. Malka wanted to know why we couldn't have a special gathering. Not in the dining room—with everyone—but just for 'us.'

Had they asked, the answer to their querulous questions would have been that the woman from Jewish Family Services, the agency that provided the matzoh and gefilte fish, the dreidels for Purim, and the menorah for Chanukah, had recently died, and the Jews no longer had a representative on the holiday planning staff.

So, they schemed. But not with one another, which might have proven successful. They schemed separately.

Shirley's group called for a meeting with Alysha, the head of activities, to create a dinner on Saturday night, which involved adding roast chicken and chicken soup and placing boxes of matzoh on the tables. Malka, who didn't have a group, met with

Chuck, the head of food services, to plan a gathering with gefilte fish, chopped liver, and macaroons. She wanted to be with the Jews, just the Jews, which meant gathering in the café on Sunday afternoon.

The tension around Passover observance had historic roots. Malka saw herself as the leader of the Jewish community, and because she was the one who put in all the work to create the schmoozes and services, she felt that residents should not only leave her alone to arrange things as she thought best, but appreciate her for doing whatever that was.

To make matters more complicated, during COVID, the year before I arrived, when residents were confined to their apartments, Malka had hollered at Chuck, then a staff member she felt was being less than attentive to her daughter who had come to drop off a meal for her housebound parents. Nothing was resolved and bad feelings were firmly planted on both sides. But he is the person with whom she had to negotiate.

Shirley was equally certain of her authority and would tolerate no disruption of her Saturday dinner plans.

"So, what's the problem? I arranged for a little extra on the table: roast chicken, some potatoes, a nice soup, a piece of matzoh, and maybe a salad. That's the least they can do for us after all the rent we pay. And I don't want to hear another word."

I was caught between Malka, for whom I played second banana, and Shirley, who saw us as soul sisters because of our geographic proximity. For Malka, the fact that Jews were given the Torah and told to live by its precepts was the central truth of her life. She is kind. And welcoming. Just so long as she's the Moses to the tribe. But as her mind continued to evaporate, and she stopped short mid-sentence, looking around helplessly, I was the one who whispered the word she was reaching for. This was her fiefdom, and I would do nothing to disrupt that.

Neither Shirley nor Malka were skillful negotiators. They announced what they wanted, sometimes smilingly, sometimes firmly. Then, they crossed their arms and waited. But there was a need to negotiate with a staff member in charge with whom there was an unpleasant history. These past disagreements did nothing to improve communication, resulting in an aggravated Malka calling Chuck stupid. In public. That did it. The battle lines were drawn.

On the Saturday side, "Did you hear what she called Chuck? What gives her the nerve to talk to him like that?"

On the Sunday side, "If you don't insist on what you want, they'll just run over you. I wouldn't be surprised if there were anti-Semitic people on the staff, but I'm not naming names."

I didn't want Passover to be centered on fighting over what and where we ate. But it was. This would be my first seder since Marcia had died, the holiday when she convened a dozen women in a gathering modeled after the Seder Sisters in New York. With her guidance, a wide range of women gathered; traditional, pagan, renewal, non-believers, activist, and cultural Jews. There was space for all of us and how or if we believed and practiced. Each year we created a sense of wholeness that emerged from our disparate religious/spiritual selves. It had been a glorious moveable feast, a high point of my Jewish life. One year later, I was witnessing a fight, ostensibly about what and where they were going to eat a Passover meal, but more deeply rooted in their need to be taken seriously.

Over the past six months, I had become seen as a good facilitator, a bigshot even. I feared that if I didn't take the reins of these warring factions and fashion something that at least resembled what I needed, I would be listening to women reminiscing about their brisket and charoset recipes, the triumphs of their grandchildren, and details about their extended families. There would be memories of seders led with hasty formality by an authoritative grandfather and beaming grandmother, of their domestic altar overflowing with lovingly prepared holiday meals, and the exuberance of grandchildren fooling around and not paying attention, much as they did, decades before.

As the impartial arbiter who might bring peace to the warring factions, I facilitated multiple meetings with both Shirley and Malka over mugs of Sanka and plastic cups of Sprite, which led to my creating the third alternative—the one I wanted. There would be a Saturday dinner meal modification assuring Shirley that she had, once again, saved the day. The Sunday café gathering and schmooze allowed Malka to sit with the half dozen people who arrived to tell seder stories, which she saw as a success. Then, Monday would be the community seder for both groups. Desert Manor offered to supply long folding tables and chairs, paper plates, silverware, tablecloths, and pitchers of cold drinks. The rest would be up to me.

I set up the tables under the awning outside the dining room, bought tulips, matzoh, wine (kosher for a couple of the residents who wouldn't otherwise imbibe), and bunches of parsley and salt water. Each resident had four half-filled paper cups of wine or grape juice at their seat, since refilling as we moved through the

Haggadah would take both time and speed, neither of which we had. This would be an abbreviated ceremony for the believers, the non-believers, and the ones who show up because it's on the schedule. This seder wouldn't be the compromise that the Saturday and Sunday gatherings had been. This was the closest semblance of what I wanted, and providing it for them would give all of us something we wanted as well.

As is the case with all Jewish ceremonies, Passover begins with bringing in the light of the candles and offering a traditional blessing over the flames. Since no live fire is allowed, I read the *Shechiyanu* blessing (an offering of appreciation that we are alive and together in this moment).

I held up the first paper cup of wine, identifying it as the one that represented our ancestors. I asked them to think of someone they tried to honor by how they were living their lives. Names rang out in voices that were both proud and affirming as we moved around the circle, recited the blessing over the wine, and drank.

Then I raised the second. Who were your teachers, and who are you teaching about how to live a righteous life? I asked. Now that they had a sense of what to expect, the answers were a bit more elaborate. Names were augmented with which school, grade, and class, embedding that revered person in the specific details of their lives.

Breaking the middle matzoh and hiding it for the children at the table to find in exchange for a reward was a way to make the seder more entertaining for them. But as I snapped the matzoh in half, there was laughter about who would search for the *afikomen*. Even the youngest among us was too old to be searching for half a matzoh, which would involve bending, stooping, and seeing underneath chairs and tables. So, I paused for some *afikomen* memories, first when they were the youngest and had to search for it, and later, when their child or grandchild repeated the process.

At past seders, I would ask what was broken in us and why we felt the need to hide that brokenness. But being broken and hidden did not have a role in this ceremony. We were here to affirm, not to examine.

Each resident dipped the parsley into the salt water to identify the bittersweet aspect of this holiday, as I asked for the names of beloved people who were no longer here to share this moment with us. There were tears as their names were called, coupled with a sense of gratitude for having the opportunity to acknowledge their loved ones who were gone.

The third cup was to honor us, our lives, and our well-being, and the fourth focused on the future, shifting to grandchildren, nieces and nephews, and all the younger people who would carry our dreams and hopes forward.

After we completed the cups with the additional redemptive representation of Miriam and Elijah, the two hours, which was everyone's maximum attention span possible, drew to a close. My faded Jerusalem tablecloth was littered with matzoh crumbs, paper cups and plates, and spilled grape juice as the residents rose, turned towards their walkers, and thanked me.

"Next year at Desert Manor," I replied.

But there wouldn't be a next year for me. Not there.

Twenty-Six
Summer Fashion Statements

Six weeks later, the unrelenting desert summer had fully descended. Now my days were organized by how long I could tolerate being outside the air-conditioned building. I awakened at 6:00 a.m. so I could walk around the building three times to get my steps in, then completed my choreographed pool dances by 7:30, before the air was searing and made breathing difficult.

Going out for groceries required racing across the asphalt to the parking structure, waiting for the air conditioning to cool my hot car, driving to the store, and parking as close as I could. I often wished I had a disabled sticker so I could park right in front, but knowing that was both politically and morally wrong, I never pursued it, even though I guiltily wanted to.

I shopped as slowly as possible to accumulate more steps on my Apple Watch. Big box stores were perfect for wandering up and down the aisles, although eventually, I became self-conscious as the staff saw me pass by them more than a half dozen times. I didn't want to appear like a confused old lady but rather like a woman languorously deciding what she wanted.

I bought a few random items and sprinted back across the parking lot to my car which was scorchingly hot again. While I waited for it to cool, whatever comfort I had experienced from my meanderings in the store evaporated.

Back at Desert Manor, I hurried into the air-conditioned lobby, steps completed, swim accomplished, and groceries purchased. By ten am! With an entire day to fill. And so it went. Day after exhausting day.

If I had a doctor's appointment (which was the only reason I'd go out in the middle of the day), I carried an umbrella to ward off the direct sun. I imagined myself as Leslie Caron in Paris, spinning and singing her way along glorious cobblestone streets, not an eighty-four-year-old woman in sneakers trying to stay cool.

The heat required further decisions about my wardrobe. Primary was the need to cover my body in something that draped loosely over it and didn't require a bra. I had two choices. A housedress or a caftan.

Housedresses give up any pretense of fashion. They're intended to cover the body, snap shut, and let the wearer slip their feet into slippers and pad around. During my rigorous childhood training, I was taught that wearing housedresses meant you weren't taking pride in your appearance. The truth is that I no longer take very much pride in my appearance. I take pride in my health, my flexibility, and my stamina. But my appearance? Maybe just my hair and my toes.

Am I seriously going to sit in my living room (balcony out of the question, given the heat) wearing clothes? But if I don't, then a housedress feels like I'm not trying, although I'm not sure what it is I'm supposed to be trying. Women of my generation learned that it's important not to let ourselves "go," but go where? All the way to comfort? All the way to no longer caring if she ever irons anything again for the rest of her life? It feels like the game of giant steps I played as a kid. Then, whenever you took one, you were moving ever closer to the goal line. But what is the goal here?

There are a few women who wear housedresses all day, but they're on scooters, and as they whiz past, they seem briefly colorful. I suppose the decision is whether my body even needs to be decorated anymore, either to communicate to the viewer or to remind me of my younger self.

I'd always imagined that women who wore caftans were sophisticated like Auntie Mame, women who entertained covered in draped and stylish fabrics, women who would never wear a housedress in a million years. I could be like that, floating around Desert Manor in a series of elegant caftans— tremendously suave and relievedly braless. Perfect.

I used to dress carefully when going out. Hair. Face. Outfit. Yes, they were called outfits then. Shoes that had a meaningful relationship with said outfit, and a corresponding bag. While I'd always intended to wear extravagant clothing, I tended to pull back at the last minute. One exception was when I came upon a pair of size eleven knee-high black leather boots that were on sale. Of course, they were. How many women have such big feet and want knee-high boots? They were practically a steal, I told myself. I bought them, but they eventually ended up in the back of my closet, along with my other random attempts at panache, awaiting the right moment for their big reveal.

I'm a world away from imagining there would be an opportunity, or better yet, multiple opportunities, where I would wear knee-high leather boots. Instead, I am in the process of shifting from my cute shoes to sneakers and considered buying housedresses. All the sartorial trappings of my life have been simplified now. Ada and Shana would be considered snappy dressers, but for the most part here, comfort supersedes style. Ada dresses playfully and mixes color and fabric, jewelry and shoes with abandon—all topped by her purple hair. She is our Iris Apfel, Shana, our Anna Wintour. Otherwise, clothing at Desert Manor for both men and women centers around velour tracksuits in pastel colors accompanied by orthopedic Velcro strap shoes. No knee-high boots in this crowd.

I'm left with an irrelevant body of knowledge about how to be chic, tasteful, and elegant—all the forms of presentation that mattered so much to my mother. But the world has changed, and clothing signaling has moved beyond my understanding of good taste. Plaids and prints are exuberantly combined. The body as a tabula rasa upon which inscriptions of all sorts can be, and are, inscribed.

I briefly considered a little tattoo on my shoulder, the only spot on my body that isn't wrinkled, but whenever the notion of beautifying myself by sticking needles into my flesh surfaces, it evaporates when, after picking out a possible image, I get to the sticking needles part which abruptly ends my decorative ruminations.

In addition to opting for comfort over style during the desert summer months, is the fact I will have to make another decision in the fall. I've been a size fourteen for nearly fifty years, but appear to be approaching a size sixteen with all deliberate speed. I'm not all the way there; I'm in between, depending on whether the waist of my pants is loose or if I eat a big meal.

When I zip up my pants in the morning, the zipping is smooth. But once I begin the day and eat anything at all, it moves only two-thirds of the way to its goal. I went to Macy's to try on a pair of size 16 pants, which were much too loose. However, instead of calling them loose, I might consider them roomy, allowing the possibility of my body spreading comfortably into them. Undecided, I leave the pants in the dressing room, drive back, and eat an apple for lunch. I'm still hungry but haven't come to a conclusion. Am I going to fight with my body to get it to return to its familiar shape, or let it soften into something more abundant, requiring both new pants and attitude, which, when I think about it, might be a good, age-appropriate idea? I love the rounded bodies of women. What's my problem? With caftans, it's temporarily not an issue since I probably won't wear pants again for a few months, and by then, my body will have done its thing. Whatever it turns out to be.

Then there is the non-fashion-related matter of my ears. There has been an uptick in COVID cases in Phoenix, so when I leave my apartment to go into any of the common areas, I have to wear a mask that hooks over my ears. One very minor upside is that I no longer stand in front of the mirror just inside my front door and bare my teeth to be sure there is no food lodging in visible crevices since my last meal. Because it doesn't matter. My mouth is covered. My teeth could be studded with kale left over from lunch, and it would remain my gastronomic secret.

My hearing aids hook over the mask's elastic straps, with glasses resting atop the other two. My ears have to carry a lot of weight just to hear, see, and be safe. When I manage to overcome my lack of motivation, weigh down my ears with all the necessary apparatus, and go downstairs, I'm still unable to have conversations with anyone. Even with my hearing aids on high, the sounds that emerge from behind their masks are a muffled, garbled blur. With no lips to read and no point in smiling, I nod and extricate myself as soon as an opening arises.

I'm upstairs a lot. And I'm still lonely.

Part Three
Finding Home

Twenty-Seven
Released From Bondage

I told my daughters funny anecdotes about driving all the Miss Daisys and assured them I was swimming and enjoying the pleasures of my spacious balcony. I lied, and then I lied some more. But, I either underestimated them or overestimated my lying skills.

One afternoon, as we were eating Caesar salads on the patio of a restaurant in an upscale mall, Alison said, "You know, Mom, maybe Tucson would be a better fit for you." I stopped chewing. My daughters had undoubtedly rehearsed this moment together.

"What makes you say that? "I responded cautiously. "Seriously, do you think it isn't clear to both of us how wrong Desert Manor is for you? It might be a good resource when you're older and need help, but you don't belong there yet."

I don't belong there. Of course, she had added a yet, but I skipped over that and leaned towards her. "Why are you bringing up Tucson?"

"I've been down there a half dozen times and love it. The politics are more like Berkeley; it's beautiful and has a rich arts and music community. And," she added, perhaps thinking that by saying this at the end of the sentence, I wouldn't notice, "there's a bigger professional community for me there. We could find apartments as near one another as they are now. What do you think about driving down for a weekend and poking around to see what you think?"

I already knew what I thought, but having once paid the price of my impulsivity, I was hesitant to trust myself. But her enthusiasm about the possibility of a move dislodged my fear that I'd disappoint my daughters if I expressed even the mildest discontent. They had worked so hard to make this move as easy as possible for me, filling my freezer and my heart with their positivity that this would work.

"But if we do decide," I said, having already privately decided, "I wouldn't move into another residential facility. I'd get my own apartment."

"Of course, you would. That's clear to both of us. We've seen it."

They had? I'd worked so hard to put up a positive, optimistic front for them, and they'd seen right through it. Apparently, my skills at dissembling were diminishing—or maybe they had never been as good as I had imagined they were. My daughters may have been onto me for decades. That was a new thought, one I skittered past, tucking it away for later review. Instead, I said, "Sure. Let's go and see what's there."

Months earlier, on one of Alison's flights to see friends on the East Coast, she had struck up a conversation with a couple from Tucson who was so devoted and enthusiastic about their city that they might have been Chamber of Commerce employees.

Alison had been to Tucson for concerts and art shows but had never explored the city. For her, it was just a destination to drive to for cultural events. They had emailed her that they'd love to show us around Tucson whenever we both wanted to come down. And they were true to their word.

Tucson is small and beautiful, surrounded by mountains. It has progressive politics, imaginative museums and galleries, a decades-old women-owned bookstore, a nationally recognized distinct cuisine, and an active LGBTQ+ community. It is both cheaper and cooler in temperature and vibe than Phoenix.

They drove us through a range of residential neighborhoods, the university campus, downtown, past the museums, the Jewish Community Center, the residential facilities (just in case I changed my mind, which I was not going to do), took us for a splendid lunch, regaled us with the unique gastronomic history of the region, and answered all our questions with patience and a deep love of the city where they had lived and worked for forty years. When we took our appreciative leave of them and settled back in my car, Alison and I looked at each other and nodded. Tucson appeared to be the next stop in my desert wanderings.

When I left Emeryville, I longed to have the details of my life taken care of, which had turned out to be a miscalculation of epic proportions. The Sandy who had moved to Phoenix, was filled with vulnerability, loss, need, and fear for what was gone and what the future might require of her. But during the last nine months, I'd come to understand the same was true of all the residents at Desert Manor. They had simply gotten a head start on me and figured out how to make this final remnant of their lives work. We were all reaching for the same things with the resources and the history we brought. To be visible. To belong. To fill this chapter of our lives with comfort, pleasure, and connection.

Desert Manor was a conveyor belt that residents stepped on when they could no longer navigate their lives and fell off when they died. The belt was always moving, new arrivals and recent deaths colliding, residents adjusting as they adapted to the deaths of friends, and incorporated whoever appeared next. Everyone was limited by bodies and minds working less and less effectively. The women sitting on their vigilantly monitored seats at the bar and dining room tables were creating a life that was a postscript to all that had ended. This insular world was the only one they had now.

When I arrived, I didn't want to be anything like them, unable to recognize any symmetries in our lives. But now, as I prepare to leave, I can so much better appreciate how they did their best to recreate what was gone. They gravitated to the people who seemed most familiar, attended activities that provided a shape for their long days and had conversations about subjects that had been a part of their shared pasts.

My identity as a lesbian feminist and progressive Jew dissolved when I entered Desert Manor. Nothing had prepared me for the conventional mid-century heterosexual culture that had been recreated there, one where I was simply another old Jewish woman. I adapted by providing rides, creating rituals, leading schmoozes, and inviting opportunities for mothers to remember their dead. I gave what I was good at and what was needed. In return, I was appreciated for my facilitation, even as all of who I was and what I wanted and needed remained unseen.

Alison and I returned to Tucson two weeks later and began to search for our next homes. I visualized myself living in a small, charming stucco two-bedroom cottage with curved walls and terra cotta floors. There were indeed several such houses for rent, but they turned out to be on streets with too many empty lots and ill-kept houses with rusted cars on the front lawn.

I had to face the disheartening fact that I was afraid to live alone after having happily been by myself for decades. I would feel exposed and didn't want it to be easy for any "up to nogoodniks" to access my home, remembering the spring evening decades ago when I returned home from a concert to find my front door ajar, the belt from my new leather jacket abandoned on the floor, the antique jewelry my lover had given me on our wedding day gone—everything stuffed into the missing pillowcase from my bed. I was not up to a repeat of that kind of vulnerability and fear. I was too old for that.

My search shifted from charming and stucco to a secure complex in a well-populated neighborhood. I found an apartment in a newly constructed building adjacent to an old convent no longer in active use after all the sisters had either died or moved back to the motherhouse. It was filled with light and had an impressive view of the mountains. In a bit of irony that didn't escape me, the front door opened directly into the kitchen, where I would have to feed myself.

Twenty-Eight
My Going Away Party

I told Shirley and Malka I would be moving to Tucson within the month, knowing the news of my departure would make its way through the community within a day. Which it did.

Dolly wished me well, then said, "I always had a hunch you weren't gonna stay. You're not ready for a place like this."

Rivka wanted me to promise we'd stay in touch.

Dov gave me a much-too-tight and long hug, his only language.

Rosalyn forgot until Shirley reminded her.

Shana took me to her studio and gave me a poster that advertised her last big show at the community center in her small town. "Come back and see the hallways as I fill them with my pieces," she said. And me, too. OK? Come back and see me."

I entered the Cinema Room for my last Schmooze. The chairs were already in a circle, and every one of them was filled. The shelf under the movie screen was lined with trays of cupcakes and pitchers of iced tea. Everyone stopped talking and turned towards me with broad, welcoming smiles as I stood in the doorway, astonished and overwhelmed by the turnout.

The seat in front of the screen—the spot for what I always tried to call the facilitator, but they insisted upon calling the leader, was empty, waiting for me to fill it one final time. Lowering myself into the oversized chair, I looked around the circle at these familiar faces and said,

"Thank you everybody. Our lives unexpectedly and briefly bumped into one another, and I am better for each of those bumps." This got a laugh. Wanting to move off center stage, I suggested we go around the circle encouraging anyone who wanted to speak to do so. Shirley firmly nixed that idea and said,

"Since you moved in, you've always asked us to talk about our lives. So now that this is the last time we're all together, it's time you tell us about yours."

Oops. I'm on the hot seat, I thought. I had longed for their curiosity all these months, and now that I was leaving, it had finally surfaced. What do I tell them that will do justice to this moment and honor all they've revealed to me?

I decided to go for broke and tell them how I learned to be a Jewish woman.

I began in the newly minted middle-class suburb of Boston of the 1940s. I told them how I diligently read *Photoplay* and *Modern Screen, Life Magazine*, and *Ladies Home Journal* to learn how big girls dressed and acted and noticed that an important distinction appeared to be their hair color. Blondes were clearly the most valued, the most popular, and the most sought-after. Redheads were spitfires like Susan Hayward, tempestuous, easy to anger and tears. Brunettes were second best to blondes. There was never a plain blonde, but lots of plain brunettes. They laughed at that. I continued, "I thought of myself as a plain brunette but didn't notice everyone in those magazines and movies teaching me what was beautiful and desirable was white."

This was received with silence.

I told them about the lives of my parents and grandparents and how they explained that Jews had lived in shtetls but were able to leave after carefully saving their money and coming to America on ships. They worked hard and brought over all the rest of the family or, at least, as many as they could; people who were called greenhorns and slept on the living room sofa until they got a job and their own room in which to live. There was appreciative nodding.

I told them I was taught that being a Jew was dangerous and it was necessary to be very careful. This meant observing how gentiles behaved and copying them, not drawing attention to yourself, not standing out in any way, blending in, and stepping aside when necessary.

I told them that having a private home meant that my mother didn't have to smell cooking odors from other people's kitchens, even though I loved going into my grandmother's apartment building and inhaling the smells in her lobby—the browning onions, baking pies, simmering stews, and soups from all the kitchens above the central stairwell, all blending in a comforting welcome.

I told them how I'd perch at my grandmother's table, watching her create meals from when she called 'before.' In one white enamel pot were chicken feet and unhatched eggs, and in another were prunes and raisins. The floor was covered in black and white octagonal tiles she washed every day after breakfast. Just underneath the gleaming coal stove was a splash of what I had been told was borscht that had spilled years before, creating a stain that looked like blood. Overheard conversations about the Czar and the Cossacks on horseback jumbled in my mind, deepening my growing suspicion that the red stain might have something to do with being a Jew.

As she chopped and stirred, she told me about growing up in Poland, eating potatoes and turnips, sharing beds and blankets with her brothers and sisters, stories meant to remind me about how good life was in America and how blessed I was. But sharing beds and eating potatoes sounded like fun to me. And her dinners didn't require the rigorous table manners my mother insisted upon. I could just enjoy my grandma's meals however I wanted to, even making smacking sounds to show how good it was. Looking around the circle, I saw I still had everyone's full attention, so I took a breath and continued.

I told them that I overheard my mother and grandparents whispering about 'camps'—something terrifying about live bodies being stacked among cords of wood and ignited. Jews marched to the edges of pits they had dug themselves, then shot. I asked them what kind of camps they were talking about, and my mother's response was to reassure me that those camps had happened very far away and not to worry, because such a thing couldn't happen here. I did worry, though, and I knew that when I got just a little bigger, maybe when I was nine, I would go to a sleepaway camp called Cedar Crest in the New Hampshire mountains. I could tell they didn't want me to be afraid, so I didn't ask what kind of camp Cedar Crest was.

I reached for my iced coffee, took a long swallow, and looked around the circle. Nobody was moving. All eyes were fastened upon me. I kept talking. I told them about feminism and what it was like to sit in a consciousness-raising group in 1970, sharing how, thirty years earlier, I had been taught to be a Jewish girl. Subtly trained by movie magazines, radio soap operas, and popular comedians ridiculing mothers-in-law and Jewish princesses. Learned what was considered beautiful, "too much," "too loud," "too assertive," or "too demanding.". There was a correct way to be a Jewish woman: to emulate well-behaved blond non-Jewish women. Speaking mildly. Not talking with your hands. Never raising your voice.

I told them that in my forties, I was in a relationship with a woman who had been diagnosed with terminal breast cancer. During the three years before her death, we went to services at Sha'ar Zahav, a newly formed gay and lesbian synagogue. "Is there such a thing? Rosalyn blurted out. "Shh," the circle instructed.

I waited till this startling piece of information had been, at least for the moment, digested and continued. This was one of the first such synagogues in the country, created during the AIDS epidemic as a gathering place for young men who were sick and dying and for those who cared for and loved them. And there was us. We were the only lesbian couple at the beginning. Sha'ar Zahav was a community of men who had been raised in Orthodox or Conservative synagogues, then disowned by both their families and houses of worship when they came out.

My partner Barbara and I were comforted to participate in such a welcoming and learned gathering. Her bald head signaled that she, too, was facing her death, and we were lovingly folded into this melancholy refuge. We attended services and studied the history of ethical wills, Jewish mourning rituals, and the post-Holocaust view of cremation. And eventually, we began to plan her funeral. I paused, waiting for my words to be absorbed, allowing a moment to pass before continuing.

I told them how I entered the mourning period after her death, held in the embrace of a scaffolding thousands of years old. First, the week-long shiva, as I sat vacant and numb in our living room filled with friends bringing dinners, memories, and the necessary minyan for a daily prayer service, then emptying again, only to refill the next day. Only alone at night was I able to be with Barbara, moving through the apartment, remembering her, remembering us.

I waited, sensing everyone lost in their translations of that first week, that ache of fresh loss. Rosalyn blew her nose; Rivka murmured something to herself. I let the silence extend a bit before going on. The end of the seven-day *Shiva* period moved into the thirty days marked by *Sloshim* when the tradition teaches that the mourner begins to re-emerge from the centrality of their grief. I had become a practicing Jew, and my first practice was to grieve. I looked around the circle for signs of restlessness, anything indicating I should wrap it up. But there wasn't. They wanted more.

I told them how I began to study, attending prayer services, reading the weekly Torah portion, exploring the Midrashic and mystical interpretations of the text, and attending classes three or four times a week—my immersion into this endless sea of knowledge and history becoming the most compelling part of my life.

I eventually became a part of Chochmat Ha Lev, which means wisdom of the heart, a synagogue where meditation balanced all the words Jews had been writing and speaking for thousands of years. I was learning that there is wisdom in silence and began to sit quietly every day, stilling my mind and listening to my own heart.

I told them that my life in this moment is embedded in the identity and practice that connects me to my history and my understanding of how to live with kindness, patience, discernment, and love—always, always love.

There was silence. Then Rosalyn got up and started to clap. Then Rivka. Soon, everyone who could get to their feet did until the rhythm of their applause began to slow. After everyone settled back in their chairs, I told them how moved and appreciated I felt, thanking them for receiving my history with such openness.

Then I asked for questions, questions I would answer. Whatever they were.

Ada raised her hand and said, "What do your daughters think about your life?"

I remembered the two of us sitting on my sofa as she told me about her son, who had taken his life. I would respond with the same honesty she had offered me.

"I was a complicated mother. My daughters were proud of me, felt neglected by me, and were protective, aware of how hard I worked to keep our lives together. There were too many moments they didn't feel chosen as my number one priority, which was painful and disappointing for them."

Then Dov spoke, his word tentative, unlike his usual bombastic certainty. "What do you think is going to happen to us if everybody decides to be Jewish in their own way? Don't we have to try to be Jewish all together?"

I answered carefully, understanding the fear underlying his question.

"I think we are being Jewish all together. There have always been Jews who worship and believe differently. Eat differently. Sing different songs. We're American Jews in 2022 who are trying to keep the love and the practice of Judaism a part of the lives of young people. We don't want them to drift away from the tradition, so we are making the tradition more open and welcoming to them."

He nodded, understanding that this was, in fact, what was already happening.

Then Malka got up, preparing to resume her familiar leadership position, and made a slow circle to look at everyone before she spoke.

"I want you to understand that I won't be Sandy. Nobody can be Sandy. But I will do my best to make both our Schmooze and Friday services a good environment for everyone."

Then abruptly, she sat down. Benny reached over and took her hand. After a long pause, Rosalyn said, "You brought my son back. I tried to let him go, but I didn't have to. I can have him with me now. Thank you."

Rivka gave me a paper mâché tiara because she said I was like the Jewish queen of Desert Manor.

And then it was over. Cupcakes were eaten, and hugs were given. We were all tired. It was nearly four, and my farewell party had begun at one. As we made our way to the elevator, we smiled, no more words necessary. They had all been said.

Epilogue

In 1904, when my grandfather arrived in America, he found factory work stitching garments from scraps of cloth, combining them into dresses, paid by the number he could complete in a ten-hour day. His new life was assembled in fragments as well. He attended the Yiddish theater every Sunday to feed his eager heart and mind. He spent Shabbat afternoon with his daughters, in whom he instilled a love of learning. He adored his wife. They had been sweethearts since they were children. He joined men in the neighborhood once or twice a week in the evening with whom he argued Talmud/Torah. His was a rich and variegated life, carefully constructed from the options available to him.

Like him, I need to do my own piecework now. My life in the Bay Area emerged from decades of living in overlapping communities of women who wrote, organized, prayed, and studied together. As I begin my life in Tucson, I return to my grandfather's teachings. "There are few answers in our lives, *maidele*. There are only better questions, and there are choices."

It was up to me to make choices now, ones that would assemble the pieces of this next chapter of my life.

I began by googling Senior Pride, an organization for LGBTQI+ folks. Scanning their website, the seniors in question appeared to be in their energetic seventies. Although I suspected those were the organization's most photogenic representatives, I trusted there were other older, less spritely members—at least, I hoped there were.

While my senior identity is just a few decades old, my lesbian self is the center from which I have lived, imagined, and loved for over fifty years. I missed being with old lesbians. Missed the shorthand we spoke with one another.

I suspected I was romanticizing my longing, but my nine months at Desert Manor had left me full of hunger—the kind that was filled with memories of the years when second-wave feminism was taking shape around me, remembering how I awakened every morning with exhilaration and a sense of possibility. I had never felt so alive as I did in those early generative days.

What constituted the lesbian self I was bringing into this new landscape? I was an old lesbian, a Jewish lesbian, a political lesbian, and a writing/reading lesbian. These would be my scraps, each containing its own richness, pieces that I'd blend into the shape of this new life.

I felt vulnerable, hopeful, and oddly shy. I said yes to everything, asked women for coffee dates, and accepted invitations after potlucks or workshops. To them, I added the rich landscape of Zoom, where I accessed author talks, synagogue services, and Jewish study classes. Each morning, I listened to podcasts providing erudite political conversations to accompany my walks around my beautiful new neighborhood.

A world was taking shape around me, with space for me. All of me. My nine months at Desert Manor evaporated in the rearview mirror like a mirage. I'm probably one of the oldest Senior Pride-ers. We are culturally varied, in various states of health and resources, and have all lost beloveds. All that comes with the territory of aging.

But we are something else. We are queer. For much of our lives, we have been seen as other, troubled, dangerous, or as a curiosity. The world has changed because of our groundbreaking beginnings and the continuing efforts of the generations that follow us. We came from a period when we had to learn to be proud. To actively practice our self-love. To insist on ourselves with our families. We speak a particular shorthand, shaped by our lives as queer in mid-century America. There is a triumph in how we live because it was such an uphill battle for so many of us.

I could not have imagined the words Senior and Pride joined together to define a community when I was a young lesbian. There were some elders, of course, and we admired them and took every opportunity to thank them for their contributions to our liberation. Still, they were larger-than-life exceptions, not everyday people like us.

Senior Pride represents a triumphant expression of our activism. It is not the outcome of a dramatic campaign like marriage equality, child custody, employment opportunities, or respectful and appropriate medical care, but the profound simplicity of an inclusive and supportive community in a midsized city in the southwest.

I sit on a much smaller balcony now, one with no pigeons and a glorious view of the mountains and the astonishing sunrises. I am an 86-year-old Jewish lesbian feminist, one who reads and writes, who prays and asks questions, and one who tries to make the world I'm in just a little bit better. After these long months of wandering, I have found my new home.

Acknowledgments

This book centers on a tumultuous eighteen months in my life. My thanks extend from the friends who released me from the decades we shared in the Bay Area with generosity and support as I made my way to what I thought would be my future, to those who, nine months later, welcomed me to Tucson.

Jane Ariel, Lorraine Bonner, Sandy Boucher, Evan Blumensweig, Dee Brown, Laurie Chaitkin, Elana Dykewomon z//l, Marinell Eva, Karen Erlichman, Marcia Freedman z//l, Nan Gefen, Jan Holmgren, Donna Korones, Naomi Newman, Eva Pettersson, Francis Reid, Penny Rosenwasser, Penelope Starr, Nancy Stoller, Rochelle Towers.

Retha and Jim Davis, the enthusiastic Tucson welcoming committee who introduced me to the city; Penelope Starr, who accompanied and encouraged me as I entered it; Lavina Tomer and Joyce Bolinger, who opened their hearts to me; and Senior Pride, the cushion upon which I came to rest.

Nan Gefen, Frances Reid, Donna Korones, Penelope Starr, and Miriam Black read every word in this book dozens of times, keeping me honest, motivated, and always encouraged. Thank you.

Thank you to Ian Henzel of Rattling Good Yarns, who understands the necessity and urgency of publishing the stories of LGBTQI+ writers. He is a visionary who never missed an errant comma or semi-colon and was an invaluable presence both to me and this book.

About the Author

Sandra Butler is Old, Jewish, and Queer. All the rest is commentary.

If you are interested in commentary, her website is sandrabutler.net

Right now, she is 86 years old, standing alongside and grateful for the generations of women putting their younger, non-arthritic shoulders to the wheel as they work to create the world we need to live in, working on her next book, delighting in the richness of her life in Tucson, and hoping not to fall.

Sandra Butler, photo by Alison Butler

9 781955 826662